GROWING UP IN MISSISSIPPI

Growing Up in Mississippi

Edited by Judy H. Tucker and Charline R. McCord

Foreword by Richard Ford

UNIVERSITY PRESS OF MISSISSIPPI ❖ JACKSON

www.upress.state.ms.us

The University Press of Mississippi is a member
of the Association of American University Presses.

Copyright © 2008 by University Press of Mississippi
Manufactured in the United States of America

First printing 2008

Library of Congress Cataloging-in-Publication Data

Growing up in Mississippi / edited by Judy H. Tucker and Charline R. McCord;
foreword by Richard Ford.
    p. cm.
  ISBN 978-1-934110-71-3 (cloth : alk. paper) 1. Mississippi—Biography—Anecdotes. 2. Youth—Mississippi—Biography—Anecdotes.
3. Mississippi—Social conditions—20th century. I. Tucker, Judy H. II. McCord,
Charline R.
  CT243.G76 2008
  976.2063092—dc22

                         2007045825

British Library Cataloging-in-Publication Data available

Contents

Richard Ford

Influence: A Flight of Fancy

Richard Ford was born in Jackson, Mississippi, in 1944, and attended public schools there. He is the author of nine books of fiction, including the trilogy, *The Sportswriter*, *Independence Day*, and *The Lay of the Land*. His novels and stories and essays have been translated into twenty-three languages, and he is a frequent contributor to the *New Yorker* and to the *New York Times*. He lives in East Boothbay, Maine, with his wife Kristina Ford.

I suppose it's the writer part of me that thinks identifying influence (knowing the forces that act on us to bring about our behavior) is not a simple matter, since doing so concerns itself with understanding why we do what we do. And we all know that's never simple. I'll give you an example from Mississippi, in the 1940s, one that took place on North Congress Street in Jackson, when I was somewhere beneath the age of six. My father was a salesman who traveled for a living and was home only on weekends. My mother and I—this is a polite way of saying it—were "alone together a lot," each of us fairly volatile of temperament, each constantly feeling a sense of "newness" toward the other (my parents were "older" and otherwise childless). One day my mother and I were in the front yard of our house there on Congress, doing what I don't remember, except that my mother got exercised about something I did or was doing—something aggravating. And suddenly she just started running—running away. She ran right out of our yard, in her housedress, ran straight across the playground at

Davis School next door, and utterly disappeared around the back of that red brick building. I, at my small age, just stood and stared as she went out of sight. I didn't know where she was going, or exactly why. Though I certainly believed something I'd done had been the cause of her sudden fleeing, which was very dramatic. And most importantly I didn't know if she'd ever be back. (She did come back, after a while. I don't remember how long a while.) But I remember that day, that sudden flight, her sense of (it must've been) entrapment, my own child's feeling of dismay and responsibility and fear. I remember it in my mind's eye and in my same heart to this very minute. It might've happened yesterday. And because I tell it now, I realize that it goes on happening.

But. What caused that to happen? And what did its happening thereafter cause? I think of myself as having been a much-loved child. I don't know what was going on in my mother's brain then. I've gone forward from that day in the '40s to live a reasonably productive life. My mother and my wife and I were extremely close all the years of my mother's life. I loved her, I miss her to this day, twenty-six years after her death. And yet here's this indelible Technicolor memory of her being driven away—by me, a small child. Her *only* child. How do I account for that—in her or in myself? And beyond that, what was that particularly frightening moment-of-childhood's *influence* on me? Did my wife and I decide, in part, not to have children based on that searing memory of my mother fleeing, the thin hem of her dress flapping in the air, her arms swinging as she ran? Am I, because of this unsettling event, more than usually fearful of loss and therefore not so easily given to intimacy? Is the imponderableness of all that—and more—the reason I'm a writer? (because so much needs explaining). Is Mississippi involved in any of that? After all, my parents were Arkies. They'd moved to Jackson only the year before I was born. No one felt especially "at home" in Mississippi. Indeed, I was the only certifiable Mississippian among the three of us. How can any of this stuff-of-life be made to make any sense at all?

Set out this way, influence—the business of why we do what we do, why we are the ways we are—instantly becomes a good deal less than obvious, and never simple. At least to me it does. Thinking about these questions, I don't know their answers. I might just as well say "everything causes everything." And if I have to address something as neatened-up and tied in a bow as: *What's Mississippi's influence on me,* I have to admit that the facts themselves, as in my childhood memory, are only one element in understanding influence; and that where the facts stop but important curiosity persists, or where the facts get congested and too numerous to make a clear picture, then the imagination (mine does, anyway) takes over. And of course maybe, all these years later, I only dreamed that my mother ran away across the Davis School playground. Maybe it never happened. So, there's that to factor in, too.

And maybe, of course, my mind's just congested and always has been. Maybe *that's* Mississippi's fault . . . I mean, its influence. Literature—imaginative writing, made-up stuff that asks our attention because the made-up stuff's better, more plausible, prettier than life-as-lived—is an effort to provide an order when the natural accumulation of life's facts and reasoned explanations and memories and beliefs and dreams just gets to be too much and threatens to overpower us and make us think our life, or even life in general, is an un-pretty muddle we don't like and don't want to notice very carefully anymore, so that we just snooze away at football on Sunday, or else go to church, or both. Is that why the NFL's on Sunday? As spiritual backup (or antidote) for the sermon at First Presbyterian? Are any of these *influences?*

Ascribing influence—to a person or a place or a wound suffered or a bad marriage or a book we read—can, of course, often just be a way of shirking responsibility for our private behavior ("I moved around a lot when I was grown because my father was a traveling salesman"). Or it can be a form of wish fulfillment ("my father forced me to do yard work when I was a boy, and that's why I can't go near a lawn-mower now that I'm an adult"). We invent our influences quite often to suit ourselves and our selves' needs—which might be to make our subsequent behavior seem more important or unassailable. I mean, it's hard to tell someone who *thinks* (or at least alleges) that he was *influenced* by the fact that he was the grandson of the last Civil War veteran in east Mossback County and therefore he harbors certain objectionable racial attitudes—hard to tell him that he *wasn't* influenced that way. How would we know? How does influence work, when you get right down to it? I'm not sure. But it rarely works as mechanistically as, say, a hammer "influencing" a nail to penetrate a prime piece of pine planking. I sometimes think that Mississippi influenced me by so insisting that Mississippi *was* an influence that I ran away (like my mother) across many state lines just to prove that the accident of birth was *not* as powerful as my own private acts of choosing. However, I'm not sure that's true. I made it up.

I know I'm evading the subject—or at least I'm not talking about it the way I was intended to. I can't help myself. My mind seems to be teeming with influences now. I can't choose just one and be happy with it or think it's enough. Maybe, then, that's my biggest influence: me, myself, my own congested brain that won't let the obvious, the conventional, be enough—won't even let *influence* mean what it wants most easily to mean.

The best I can do to establish influence about anything more complicated than a pine plank—for example, why my mother ran away and its aftermath—would be to make up a story about it; a piece of fiction, whose shape and tone and arc and temperament and sympathies and preconceptions and storage of experience would be generous enough to include as much as I know and can make fit, and that I think is good and true. *That* would be one effort—my best one—to account for *influence.* I grew up not far from Eudora Welty, after all, and in a time when Faulkner was alive, and Walker Percy was in New Orleans writing *The Moviegoer,* and Ellen Douglas was in the Delta, Barry Hannah lived in Clinton—and, of course, Margaret Walker Alexander was across town. Imagination, its sanctioning force field for organizing and giving language to the mute and unorganized, was the susurrus in the air I breathed in when I was growing up in Mississippi. That might've been my influence. Or maybe all these worthy writers' minds were just congested the way mine was, and we all took the same path by coincidence and out of desperation and yearning. Maybe Mississippi had something to do with it, maybe nothing. If I said it did, I'd be making that up, too. Maybe we'd all have done the same if we'd lived in Iowa. To my mind, though, it matters far less what influences us than that we take responsibility for what we do—as in my case, for what we write, how we write it. That's what authorship is. It's different from influence. And you can practice it anywhere.

Charline R. McCord and Judy H. Tucker

Judy H. Tucker *and* Charline R. McCord

Introduction

Judy H. Tucker, a native Mississippian, is a freelance editor living in Jackson. In 2007 she was the recipient of a Mississippi Arts Commission Literary Arts Fellowship.

Charline R. McCord, a resident of Clinton, Mississippi, was born in Hattiesburg and grew up in Laurel, Mississippi, and Jackson, Tennessee. She holds a Ph.D. in English from the University of Southern Mississippi and bachelor's and master's degrees in English from Mississippi College, where she won the Bellamann Award for Creative Writing and edited the literary magazine.

Together they have edited a series of Christmas books—*A Dixie Christmas, Christmas in the South, A Very Southern Christmas, Christmas Stories from Mississippi*—and coming in 2008 *Christmas Stories from the South's Best Writers.*

A Mississippi childhood bestows unique gifts upon its own. The most fortunate of children take from it the stuff of legend—generations of deeply rooted family ties, the space and time for contemplation, a connected community, an awareness and an awe of the natural world, the scars left by a conflicted history, the blessing of a rich soil, the curse of an unequal bounty, and a deep and abiding faith in a power greater than themselves. Coming from this exotic mixture, a child is marked by influences both within and without himself or herself.

In his foreword Richard Ford dissects the very nature of influence. He has taken his topic apart at the seams and turned it inside out, examining it from all sides and underneath, then reassembling it in a way that engages all of us. The native Mississippian—Pulitzer Prize–winning novelist, short story writer, essayist—tackles the subject using the inimitable style of a master of introspection and of his trade.

This collection of essays, arranged chronologically, celebrates a diverse group of Mississippians whose achievements cover a wide range of accomplishments. It also represents the many opportunities that our state nourishes. Each of the essayists, in his or her unique way, provides a worthy role model. Governor William Winter writes about growing up on a farm in Depression-era Mississippi. The great leader that he would become is foreshadowed by the thoughtful boy, an only child, who spent time in the company of the children of the tenants on the farm and his pets and the farm animals. There was ample time in the young boy's life for introspection and observation, time to develop an appreciation for life in all its variety. It is easy to see how this would become the basis of a personal philosophy that would lead Governor Winter toward a life of selfless public service at a crucial time in our state's history.

We found a panoply of talent, generosity, ingenuity, and drive— the writers who chronicle the history of our lives, the educators who interpret and teach it, the artists who preserve its likeness, the songwriters who celebrate it, the ministers who find the meaning in it, the volunteers who share it, the businessmen who package and deliver it, those in the justice system who protect it—the tapestry of our lives.

This collection of essays attempts to shed light on the influences that forged the character of these productive citizens, and guided them as they made their way in life. As each writer talks about his or her own childhood, patterns inevitably emerge. You will find repeated references to their communities, churches, teachers, parents, and grandparents. They also acknowledge the sway of the natural world in all its beauty and benevolence as well as its power and danger.

Clifton Taulbert listened to tales of "the great flood of '27" as told by his father and his grandfather. He makes the case that for his generation Hurricane Katrina will become "the great flood." Don Peterson remembers a special wild place near his home in Grenada where he found an arena to act out his daydreams. In the recollection of his solitary play in "Spooky Canyon," there is an eerie feeling, perhaps a premonition, that he would spend his career pushing at the limits of the heavens as a test pilot and an astronaut. Jimmy Buffett, born in Pascagoula, raised on the shores of Mobile Bay, speaks movingly of his discovery of the healing power of the salt water of the Mississippi Sound.

Lorian Hemingway, who spent many of her formative years in Jackson, wrote about her lifelong affinity for fish: how she loved to fish or just keep company with fish, as when she discovered a pond of mysterious albino catfish in rural Hinds County. Did she come by it naturally by way of her Hemingway genes? Had she read her grandfather's classic, *The Old Man and the Sea*? She doesn't tell us. Her focus is firmly on fish. Actor/playwright John Maxwell also writes about a memorable fishing trip on the Big Black River with his father.

Watercolorist Wyatt Waters, whose art graces the cover of this book, gives credit to his mother and his first art teacher, Miss Rose. Noel Polk talks about the study of the English language as a preparation for the ministry. At a crossroads, he chose to teach instead of preach in large part because of a high school English teacher whom he portrays in exquisite detail. Judge Fred Banks salutes the teachers who prepared him for his future as a supreme court justice and a lawyer in private practice.

As it is with Polk's eloquent essay, church and faith, if not the central theme, is certainly a nuance to many of the pieces. The strictures of the church, her family, and community compelled Elizabeth Spencer to examine the dogma, leaving her with an independence that is always reflected in her award-winning literary work. Keith Tonkel, who would spend his adult life in the service of the church, writes about his stalwart grandfather for whom he was named. Edward Cohen describes the temple as a fortress in which he felt completely safe and at home as he lived his life among a Christian majority.

Journalist and editor Sid Salter details the unique joy of sharing life with a twin, and the devastation of losing her. TV anchor Maggie Wade writes with pure pleasure about growing up in the midst of a large, extended family. Gwen Gong, now an educator in Hong Kong, recounts the experience of working and learning in her daddy's store, which sat squarely on the line between the black and the white communities in the Delta town of Boyle.

Constance Slaughter-Harvey's essay about her family's cross-country travels is a history lesson, as well as the study of a little girl with a steely intellect intent on making a mark on that history. Novelist Carolyn Haines explains how her newspaper family pointed her toward her chosen profession.

Ellen Douglas allows us a glimpse of a magical childhood spent among the storied mansions of Natchez. She romped through the primeval woods of The Forest and played among the rafters of the Moorish castle known as Longwood where her family lived for a season. Sela Ward writes about the protection of her cul-de-sac in Meridian, while Robert St. John recalls childhood memories from a simpler time in Hattiesburg. Chancellor Robert Khayat writes about his hometown of Moss Point and a piano teacher who taught him about more than musical scales.

Alberto Mora, citizen of the world, retired general counsel to the U.S. Navy, now chief legal counsel for Wal-Mart International and winner of a 2006 Profile in Courage Award, writes movingly about becoming a Mississippian, and points to a certain intersection in North Jackson as his "emotional ground zero." Newspaper publisher George Riggs describes an unexpected course correction in his life; the year was 1968 and the war in Vietnam was raging.

From her earliest years Libby Aydelott learned the value of volunteering. Throughout her life she has offered her many talents and her limitless enthusiasm to a grateful community. As a young boy in Mount Olive, Ralph Eubanks often went to work with his father, a Negro County Agent, who offered his help to both races in solving problems with their livestock and their crops. The help was given with quiet dignity and received with gratitude.

Perhaps no art form is more mysterious in its origin, or as evocative in its effect, as music. Our state is blessed with a wide variety of composers, singers, stylists, and instrumentalists. As you might expect, musicians write about their introduction to music, and often that came in the form of church music. Composer and conductor Samuel Jones remembers attending all-day singings with "dinner on the grounds" at rural churches in the Delta. The "shaped notes" of sacred harp hymns haunted his memory and influenced his composition as he wrote his most performed work, *Let Us Now Praise Famous Men.*

From his earliest days, B. B. King heard the moans and rhythms of the "shouters" echoing across the Delta cotton fields as they went about their labor. "Some of this music you might call the blues," he writes. You might call that understatement, in the same way it is understatement to say that B. B. King continues to shape the world of rhythm and blues.

Songwriter and performer Jim Weatherly has a list of memories of favorite stars that reads like a roll call from the Rock and Roll Hall of Fame: Elvis Presley, Carl Perkins, Johnny Cash, and others, but he also acknowledges the influence of gospel music in his work. The Pontotoc native, now living in Nashville, draws heavily on his past when he creates. His songs have enshrined the memories from his youth in the hearts and minds of those who shared the experience of a Mississippi childhood.

This book begins with the memories of one of our greatest statesmen, Governor William Winter, and closes with Jerry Rice, our most celebrated football player. Rice, with three Super Bowl rings in his possession, is considered the greatest wide receiver in the game. When he first stepped onto the playing field as a sophomore at B. L. Moor High School, he began preparing for a long, successful career in the NFL. There in the tiny Delta town of Crawford, he learned lessons that led to a legendary sports career and to a considered, balanced, and altruistic life after his glory days in football were over.

Growing Up in Mississippi intends to leave a record of those times, fast changing. While we examine the influences of their childhoods, we want to recognize and honor the work of these talented and dedicated Mississippians who inform and enrich our lives, and whose stories bear telling, contemplating, and retelling.

GROWING UP IN MISSISSIPPI

William F. Winter

William F. Winter, born in 1923, served as governor of Mississippi from 1980 to 1984. He has been a longtime advocate for public education, racial reconciliation, and historic preservation. An attorney in the firm of Watkins, Winter & Stennis in Jackson, he is a graduate of the University of Mississippi School of Law. He is married to the former Elise Varner, and they have three daughters and five grandchildren.

The most enduring memories of my childhood center around my life on the Grenada County farm where I grew up during the Great Depression. My family's modest home stood on a gently rising dome of land a half-mile off the county road. It was shaded by century-old oak trees and smaller cedars. Looking east from the screened front porch, one could see on a clear day the plumes of smoke rising from the mills in Grenada ten miles away. It was on that porch on countless summer evenings, before electric lights and radio and telephone intervened, that my father and mother and I would sit talking in the gathering darkness and my father would regale me with stories of his own boyhood on that same farm in the years following the Civil War and of the experiences that his father had had as a sixteen-year-old Confederate soldier.

My playmates were for the most part black children my own age who lived on the farm and with whom I played games, fished in the nearby lakes, and swam in the sandy creeks that crossed the farm. It was this array of simple childhood experiences that for me, as for all of us for better or worse, did so much to shape my personal values and my later life.

Of all my memories of those times none remain more vividly with me than those of my association with my animal pets—small animals, big animals, animals that lived with me and were part of my very being. There were first of all the usual dogs and cats that were common to the experiences of almost every child in those days.

When I was five years old, my father came home from town one afternoon with an Airedale puppy which became the center of my affection. I named this dog Andy from one of my favorite comic page characters, Andy Gump, and he thus joined Puddinhead, the cat, which was already a part of our household.

It was from these animal associates that I learned some of my first lessons about life's minor joys and tragedies. As Andy grew into a handsome and stalwart adult, I found in him both a virtually inseparable companion and my defender from any harm that might come my way. We shared the same birthday, and as he and I approached our birthdays together—his first and my sixth—we both fell ill. I went down with a case of influenza, and even though flu was not to be taken lightly, it was obvious that Andy had something far more serious. Lying in my bed, I watched him outside my window as he writhed, choking and gagging from the mysterious disease that had suddenly seized him. There was no veterinarian to call even if we had had a telephone. My father shared my anguish. The next morning the gallant little dog was dead, and for the first time in my young life I came face to face with the trauma of losing a friend.

Andy was the first in a long line of canine members of our family—a succession that continues with ever-increasing affection until the present time. They have encompassed the entire range of the species, from the most common and ordinary mutts to those of impeccable breeding with ancestors bearing imperious names like Baron Hans von Schnauzer. Their names served as a commentary on the dogs themselves.

After Andy's death it was obvious that steps had to be taken to fill the void. One of our neighbors had gotten word of the loss and within weeks brought to our house one of a litter of black and white collie puppies. I noticed that this little dog seemed to sip his milk from a saucer rather than lapping it with his tongue. Thus, we gave him the name "Sip." No dog was ever quicker to learn—to herd cows, to fetch sticks, to guard the house. He particularly liked to go to school with me, following me on the days when we walked to the little one-room school where my mother taught, but never missing an opportunity to ride with my mother and me in our T-Model Ford. On the mild fall days he would lie just outside the schoolhouse on the soft grass, but on the cold wet winter mornings he would stretch out in front of the big wood-burning stove while the children's lessons proceeded around him.

The pleasure which he derived from riding in an automobile proved to be his undoing. An unstintingly friendly and trusting creature, he knew no strangers, especially if they had a car. He would ride with anyone. Those few neighbors who possessed automobiles would pick him up as he walked along the road. He was a frequent visitor in their homes. We accepted his wide-ranging habits of consorting with his friends. One spring day, however, just past his first birthday, he did not show up at home. No one in the neighborhood could provide a clue. We never saw him again. And so little more than a year after we lost Andy to an unforgiving illness, we lost Sip to an unknown but, we hoped, a kinder fate. By age seven I had seen two of my adored dog friends snatched away.

Again the same gracious neighbor came to our aid. Within days of Sip's disappearance, we were presented with a virtual carbon copy. We named him Sip, too, and he would be the dog with whom I would grow up and who would provide me with some of my unforgettable memories.

If Sip the First was a great cow dog and a neighborhood gadabout, Sip the Second was the athlete. As I grew older and began to fancy myself the next Red Grange, I needed a playing partner to help me hone my gridiron skills. Sip was the obvious choice. A favorite uncle had given me a battered old football that he had acquired when he was a student at Ole Miss. Its frayed webbing made it just right for Sip to hold in his teeth.

And so as the leaves began to turn in the fall of the year when I was in the fourth grade, Sip and I devised a game of football on the broad expanse of grassy lawn in front of our house. I would place Sip on one side of the yard, and, with my football, I would go to the other end some twenty yards away. I would then proceed to punt the football with all of the force of my sixty-odd pounds to the fleet-footed Sip, who would run it down, pick it up by the loose webbing, and then attempt to run it back through my end of the field for a touchdown. My obvious assignment was to tackle him. To his credit he never tried to show me up by running to the sidelines. He would come straight at me as if to say, "We'll go mano a mano," and even though I had a slight weight advantage, he would more often than not break my tackle and dash through for a score. Not fully understanding the rules, though, he would then rush back toward the opposite end of the field daring me to tackle him again.

Miraculously there were no injuries in those games, even though we played them endlessly in the late afternoons until my mother would call me to supper. Sip seemed to enjoy them as much as I did. Since I weighed only slightly more than a hundred pounds when I entered high school, that was about the only competitive football that I ever got to play.

As I grew older, Sip was joined by the likes of Sir Patrick Spens, a little terrier named for a character out of English literature that I had taken a fancy to. As is the natural tendency of many terriers, he was a very intense, highly charged little dog, who, unlike the laid-back, easygoing Sip, had a hair-trigger temper. My hands still bear the scars of his teeth marks as he responded violently more than once to what he perceived as my inappropriate teasing. Still he was a warm and forgiving friend who minutes after having bloodied my hand would lick it with his tongue in an obvious gesture of apology.

Perhaps Sir Patrick's most noticeable gift to our household was his contribution of a male puppy from a litter which he had sired as a result of an arranged liaison with a lovely little neighbor dog. I gave the new puppy the most impressive name that I could think of—Napoleon Bonaparte. We called him Nap. Father and son, Pat and Nap were the dogs of my high school years and saw me off to college and to World War II. Sir Patrick did not survive the war, but Napoleon was still there when I returned from overseas. In the meantime we had acquired a collie which I gave the audacious name of Lycurgus. We got him from some friends of my father who lived in the Sparta community across the river. Somewhere I had read of a man named Lycurgus, who was the lawgiver to the Spartans of ancient Greece. I thought that since my father was in the legislature and the people of Sparta in Grenada County were his constituents, it was not inappropriate that our dog bear that honored name. I could never be certain that Lycurgus ever understood the burden that I had thus imposed on him, but so far as we knew, he never did anything to bring dishonor to the name he bore.

The dogs constituted perhaps the most important but not the only dimension of my animal world. During my middle boyhood years at different times and on occasion at the same time, I would find myself in the company of horses, cats, sheep, goats, pigs, chickens, and turkeys. They were not just nameless, impersonal, unthinking creatures to be treated with compassion. They were my friends who had real names and who had their own fascinating individual personalities.

There was, for instance, Sanford the pig. On the day that my father gave me this sandcolored little runt from a large litter that one of his sows had produced, the Memphis *Commercial Appeal* heralded the feat of a placekicker from the University of Alabama named Sandy Sanford who had kicked a last-minute field goal that enabled the Crimson Tide to go to the Rose Bowl. As an avid reader of the sports pages, I was an Ole Miss follower, but I somehow thought it fitting to name my sandy-haired porcine friend for the Alabama football star. Sanford responded to my special interest in his young life in ways that I could not have expected. In order to help him overcome his unpromising physical stature I fed him a concoction of buttermilk and ground wheat kernels called shorts. Soon my pig weighed more than his brothers and sisters, but what was equally significant and of some annoyance to my mother was Sanford's insistence on following me wherever I went—certainly to the corn crib, but also up to the steps and onto the back porch of our house and even on occasion down the road with me to the school bus. He would meet me at the front gate when I came home from school. He slept on a bed of hay under our house, sharing the facilities on cold winter nights with a resigned and patient Sip the dog.

As the months went by, Sanford, as a result of my insistence on his receiving an inordinate amount of food, was growing into a huge, ungainly, and obstreperous hog. He was making a nuisance of himself—interfering with the chickens, annoying the cows, literally throwing his weight around the barnyard. After one particularly trying afternoon when Sanford broke into my father's garden and gorged himself on an entire row of butterbeans, it was obvious that stern measures had to be taken. No longer the lovable, playful little pig that I had tenderly cared for, Sanford had become persona non grata to my parents and the other household pets. It was, in effect, time for him to go.

And so on a day later that fall when I was away at school, my father, having indicated to me that he had endured the increasingly boorish hog long enough, arranged for him to be picked up by a local livestock buyer and carted off to a fate that I could not bear to think about and that even now produces pangs of guilt for my having acquiesced in such an ignominious end for my once beloved little Sanford.

In addition to the dogs and the pig there was Cock Robin, a big boisterous white rooster, and Dizzy Dean, a colorful little bantam, who was named for another of my sports heroes. They were joined by a frizzly hen named Olive Oyl who, like her comic strip counterpart, was one of the homeliest of God's creatures. These three chickens formed a trio of barnyard entertainers who would come rushing together out of nowhere the moment I opened the back porch door. In the company of the other animals they would follow me to the building where the chicken feed was stored and gather around to catch in their beaks the grains of corn that I threw them, as they jumped above the other chickens.

There was, finally, Maggie the Goat. No account of my childhood exploits would be complete without mention of the time that I took Maggie to school on the school bus when I was in the seventh grade. It was in response to a call for a bit part in the annual senior play. They needed a goat as a walk-on character, and I volunteered Maggie for the role. I tied her to the seesaws outside the school building while I went to class. Under my direction she performed brilliantly in the play that evening, but her acting career somehow never took off after that.

These experiences left me with an affection for animals which has stayed with me all of my life. It extended to the years when my family and I were joined at the Governor's Mansion first by our little terrier, Nicky, and later by our beloved schnauzer, Toby, who learned to ride the elevator there all by himself.

Now we have Fritz, another schnauzer, who has won an even greater place in my affection. It was the intrepid Fritz, who, on a rainy evening several years ago, attacked a would-be robber who was holding our daughter, Anne, and me at gunpoint on the street in front of our home. The fearless little dog—all thirty-five pounds of him—lunged at the gunman with such ferocity that the latter retreated to his car and disappeared into the night. Thus has continued and still continues my lifelong romance with dogs and other animals who have taught me so much about life and the qualities of loyalty, love, and laughter.

Elizabeth Spencer

Elizabeth Spencer, born in 1921, is a native of Carrollton and received an M.A. from Vanderbilt. She has published nine novels, seven short story collections, a memoir, and a drama. After an extensive stay in Italy, Spencer came home to teach writing at UNC until 1992. Her honors include five O. Henry Awards, the Governor's Award for Achievement in Literature from the Mississippi Arts Commission, the PEN/Malamud Award for Short Fiction, the Award of Merit from the American Academy of Arts and Letters, and a Guggenheim Fellowship.

I t was a Sunday like no other, for we were there alone for the first time. I hadn't started to school yet, and he had finished it so long ago it must have been like a dream of something that was meant to happen but had never really come about, for I can remember no story of school that he ever told me, and to think of him as sitting in a class equal with others is as beyond me now as it was then. I cannot imagine it. He read a lot and might conceivably have had a tutor—that I can imagine, in his plantation world.

But this was a town he'd finally come to, to stay with his daughter in his old age, she being also my mother. I was the only one free to be with him all the time and the same went for his being with me—we baby-sat each other.

But that word wasn't known then.

A great many things were known, however; among them: I always had to go to Sunday school.

It was an absolute that the whole world was meant to be part of the church, and if my grandfather seldom went, it was a puzzle no

11

one tried to solve. Sermons were a fate I had only recently got big enough to be included in, but I had been enrolled in Sunday school classes since I could be led through the door and placed on a tiny red chair, my feet not even connecting to the floor. It was always cold at the church; even in summer, it was cool inside. We were given pictures to color and Bible verses to memorize, and at the end, a colored card with a picture of Moses or Jesus or somebody else from the Bible, exotically bearded and robed.

Today I might not be going to Sunday school, and my regret was only for the card. I wondered what it would be like. There was no one to bring it to me. My mother and father were not in town. They had got into the car right after breakfast and had driven away to a neighboring town. A cousin had died and they were going to the funeral. I was too little to go to funerals, my mother said.

After they left I sat on the rug near my grandfather. He was asleep in his chair before the fire, snoring. Presently his snoring woke him up. He cut himself some tobacco and put it in his mouth. "Are you going to Sunday school?" he asked me. "I can't go there by myself," I said. "Nobody said I had to take you," he remarked, more to himself than to me. It wasn't the first time I knew we were in the same boat, he and I. We had to do what they said, being outside the main scale of life where things really happened, but by the same token we didn't have to do what they didn't say. Somewhere along the line, however, my grandfather had earned rights I didn't have. Not having to go to church was one; also, he had his own money and didn't have to ask for any.

He looked out the window.

"It's going to be a pretty day," he said.

How we found ourselves on the road downtown on Sunday morning, I don't remember. It was as far to get to town as it was to get to church, though in the opposite direction, and we both must have known that, but we didn't remark upon it as we went along. My grandfather walked to town every day except Sunday, when it was considered a sin to go there, for the drugstore was open and the barbershop, on occasions, if the weather was fair; and the filling station was open. My parents thought that the drugstore had to be open but should sell drugs only, and that filling stations and barbershops shouldn't be open at all. There should be a way to telephone the filling station in case you had to have gas for emergency use. This was all worked out between them. I had often heard them talk about it. No one should go to town on Sunday, they said, for it encouraged the error of the ones who kept their stores open.

My grandfather was a very tall man; I had to reach up to hold his hand while walking. He wore dark blue and gray herringbone suits, and the coat flap was a long way up, the gold watch chain almost out of sight. I could see his walking cane moving opposite me, briskly swung with the rhythm of his stride: it was my companion. Along the way it occurred to me that we were terribly excited, and the familiar way looked new and different, as though a haze that had hung over everything had been whipped away all at once, like a scarf. I was also having more fun than I'd ever had before.

When he came to the barbershop, my grandfather stepped inside and spoke to the barber and to all who happened to be hanging around, brought out by the sunshine. They spoke about politics, the crops, and the weather. The barber, who always cut my hair, came over and looked to see if I needed another trim and my grandfather said he didn't think so, but I might need a good brushing; they'd left so soon after breakfast it was a wonder I was dressed. Somebody who'd come in after us said, "Funeral in Grenada, ain't it?" which was the first anybody had mentioned it, but I knew they hadn't needed to say anything, that everybody knew about my parents' departure and why and where. Things were always known about, I saw, but not cared about too much either. The barber's strong arms, fleecy with reddish hair, swung me up into his big chair, where I loved to be. He brushed my hair, then combed it. The great mirrors sparkled and everything was fine.

We presently moved on to the drugstore. The druggist, a small crippled man, hobbled toward us, grinning to see us, and he and my grandfather talked for quite some time. Finally my grandfather said, "Give the child a strawberry cone," and so I had it, miraculous, and the world of which it was the center expanded about it with gracious, silent delight. It was a thing too wondrous actually to have eaten, and I do not remember eating it. It was only after we at last reached home and I entered the house, which smelled like my parents' clothes and their things, that I knew what they would think of what we had done and I became filled with anxiety and other forebodings.

Then the car was coming up the drive and they were alighting in a post-funeral manner, full of heavy feelings and reminiscence and inclined not to speak in an ordinary way. When my mother put dinner in order, we sat around the table not saying very much.

"Did the fire hold out all right?" she asked my grandfather.

"Oh, it was warm," he said. "Didn't need much." He ate quietly and so did I.

On Sunday afternoons we all sat around looking at the paper. My mother had doubts about this, but we all indulged the desire anyway. After the ordeal of dressing up, of Sunday school and the long service and dinner, it seemed almost a debauchery to be able to pitch into those large crackling sheets, especially the funny papers, which were garish with color and loud with exclamation points, question marks, shouting, and all sorts of misdeeds. My grandfather had got sleepy before the fire and retired to his room, while my mother and father had climbed out of their graveside feelings enough to talk a little and joke with one another.

"What did you all do?" my mother asked me. "How did you spend the time while we were gone?"

"We walked downtown," I said, for I had been laughing at something they had said to each other and wanted to share the morning's happiness with them without telling any more or letting any real trouble in. But my mother was on it, quicker than anything.

"You didn't go in the drugstore, did you?"

And they both were looking. My face must have had astonishment on it as well as guilt. Not even I could have imagined them going this far. Why, on the day of a funeral, should they care if anybody bought an ice-cream cone?

"Did you?" my father asked.

The thing to know is that my parents really believed everything they said they believed. They believed that awful punishments were meted out to those who did not remember the Sabbath was holy. They believed about a million other things. They were terribly honest about it.

Much later on, my mother went into my grandfather's room. I was silently behind her, and I heard her speak to him.

"She says you took her to town while we were gone and got an ice cream."

He had waked up and was reading by his lamp. At first he seemed not to hear; at last, he put his book face down in his lap and looked up. "I did," he said lightly.

A silence fell between them. Finally she turned and went away.

This, so far as I know, was all.

But of the incident, that certain immunity of spirit my grandfather possessed was passed on to me. It came, I think, out of the precise way in which he put his book down on his lap to answer. There was a lifetime in the gesture, distilled, and I have been a good part of that long, growing up to all its meaning.

After this, though all went on as before, there was nothing much my parents could finally do about the church and me. They could lock the barn door, but the bright horse of freedom was already loose in my world. Down the hill, across the creek, in the next pasture—where? Somewhere, certainly; that much was proved, and all was different for its being so.

A Final Word

I was fourteen when he died. I had gone to Teoc with my aunt and uncle to spend a weekend. When we got to the house the telephone was ringing. It was my mother, telling us to return at once.

I was frightened as we drove the winding country road back to town. I remember huddling in the back seat, thinking that though my mother had not said so, we must all know what had occurred. On the front seat they were silent. I think grief was not so strong with me as fear.

I wondered later what I was afraid of. But in a way, I knew. He was the loving companion of days that would never be repeated. There have been many loves for me since then, but none quite like that. I could remember it, but not call it back. This fact, which confronted me that night, is as awesome, as fearful, as anything can get. It's enough to scare anybody to death.

From Teoc Gan once brought a pocketful of acorns from the live oaks near the house. He went around the yard in Carrollton planting all these. I was with him. I remember his bending to dig a sufficiently deep hole, dropping in the acorns, tamping the soil back over them with the tip of his cane.

Those trees now stand tall and strong around the house. It was sold after my parents' death, and though it is in the hands of good owners, I nevertheless dislike going there now that so many have passed away. But when I see those noble oaks, I am cheered. I remember the day, and that planting, and can see the yield which seems to honor it.

Ellen Douglas

Ellen Douglas (Josephine Haxton), born in Natchez in 1921, is a graduate of the University of Mississippi. Among her eight novels, *A Family's Affairs* and *Black Cloud, White Cloud* were included in the *New York Times Book Review*'s ten best of the year listings; *A Family's Affairs* received a Houghton Mifflin Fellowship; and *Apostles of Light* was a finalist for the National Book Award. *Truth: Four Stories I Am Finally Old Enough to Tell* was published by Algonquin Books of Chapel Hill in 1998, and her latest work, *Witnessing*, a collection of articles and essays, was published by University Press in 2004.

. . . let me tell you about Natchez and Longwood and The Forest. Think first, not of Tara and hoopskirts and ruthless Southern belles, but rather of churches, bells ringing for Sunday services and Wednesday night prayer meeting, of ladies and gentlemen and children in worn but respectable Sunday clothes gathering to worship God and to find some order and joy in a difficult world. Think, too, of early-twentieth-century poverty, of making do in a depression that began in the riverine South with—what? The end of the Civil War? The advent of railroads and the loss of the river as a highway? The feckless clear-cutting of that hilly land? The coming of the boll weevil in 1915? All of these. Sixty-odd years ago when I was growing up, everyone I knew went to church and almost everyone was poor. Not hungry. Not in rags (only the Negroes were in rags), but poor.

To me ours was never a doomish, a threatening poverty, but rather the comfortable limitations that may seem to a child to be—and be, at least for a while—security. In those days paint curled off my grandmothers' ceilings. Drapes had not been replaced in years. Scraps of newspaper folded into spills stood in a jar on the mantelpiece for use as matches to light my aunt's cigarettes from the fire glowing in the coal grate. (Surely there was money for matches, wasn't there, if there was money for cigarettes? Or was the jar of spills evidence of Presbyterian thrift carried to its limits?) In any event, for us children, there were books (mostly very old ones, it's true) and someone always ready to read or tell you a story. And in the country there were lakes to swim in, creeks to wade, ponds with ducks to be fed, and woods to explore.

Here, on the outskirts of the small town of Natchez, is Longwood—a wildly extravagant Moorish castle of a mansion (Nutt's Folly, people called it) left unfinished in 1861 when the Civil War broke out. No one in the Nutt family ever again had the money (or perhaps the hubris, either) to finish it. Instead, they and the subsequent descendants sold away or lost most of the land, lived on the finished ground floor, and left the top four floors (still littered with scaffolding, dried-up buckets of paint, canvas carpenters' aprons, ladders, and tools) to mice and owls and bats and children's explorations. I remember as a child climbing among the rafters and floor joists and looking out from the windowed dome over abandoned fields and shaggy lawns, over thickets of gum and locust and pecan that I knew must once have been gardens, because in their seasons I could see unkillable spirea and daffodils and crepe myrtles still blooming.

Here, too, is The Forest, another country place we occasionally visited—no more doomish or gloomish than Longwood. The main house—built by an ancestor named William Dunbar—had burned years before the Civil War, and the old carriage house had been converted into a long low cottage with a gallery across the front (as I seem to recall, although I haven't been there in more than fifty years). There in the 1930s, my great-aunt Marian Davis lived with her husband, Jamie, whom she'd married in late middle age.

I remember we especially liked going to The Forest because Jamie and Marian had a donkey they would let us ride. Hard now to think of anything less exciting—I can't remember ever being able to kick that passive beast into a trot. But ride we did. The donkey existed. My sister has a snapshot of the two of us and a cousin all sitting on him, our feet almost touching the ground. And then, when we tired of riding, while the grown-ups sat on the gallery in quiet and intimate conversation, we'd explore the ruin of the old house—nothing left but two or three crumbling columns and the half-buried foundation—and wander through the family graveyard close by.

B. B. King

B. B. King, known worldwide as the "King of the Blues," was born in 1925 on a cotton plantation in Itta Bena. From early childhood he was interested in music. One of the world's most celebrated musicians, he has released over fifty albums which mix blues, jazz, swing, pop, and gospel. He has traveled the world performing his music with his signature guitar "Lucille." *Rolling Stone* selected him as the number three greatest musician of all times. He has won fourteen Grammys and in 1987 was inducted into the Rock and Roll Hall of Fame.

The most worthwhile thing about Aunt Mima's place was her crank-up Victrola, a machine that changed my life. See, Mima was a music fan. She had the first collection I'd ever seen. She'd go into town and find records, bring 'em home, and neatly pile 'em up next to the Victrola. You'd wind up the record player like you'd wind up a watch. Her first model was a cylinder; later she got a turntable. Her 78 rpm shellac discs were shiny platters that looked like flying saucers. Aunt Mima taught me to gently put on the platter, set down the needle, and watch the turntable spin. A second passed and then—*pow!*—those beautiful scratchy sounds flew in my face, cutting right through me, electrifying my soul.

Now I'd heard shouting in the fields ever since I could remember. My daddy could sing him some blues. Big husky voice. And I had an uncle—Mama's sister's husband—called Jack Bennett. You could hear Uncle Jack singing from miles away. No matter where you went, walking behind the plow or picking cotton, you'd be hearing beautiful voices, singing about the sun high in the sky or the gathering storm clouds or the long, hard day or how good the food would taste once work was done. Seems like the songs were made up by the heart, nothing written or rehearsed, music meant to take the ache out of our backs and the burden off our brains. Some of this music you might call blues.

Blind Lemon Jefferson was as close to the field shouters as anyone else. Aunt Mima had his records, and later I learned he came from Texas. He had a big burly voice—like Daddy and Uncle Jack—and put so much feeling into his words until I believed everything he sang. He had power. Like all the great bluesmen, Blind Lemon sang for sinners. When he sang "Rabbit Foot Blues" or "That Crawlin' Baby Blues" or "Mosquito Moan," I moaned along with him. It was like him and his guitar were part of the same being. You didn't know where one stopped and the other started. Blind Lemon was strong and direct and bone-close to my home.

Lonnie Johnson was different. Mima loved Lonnie Johnson and soon I learned to love him even more. It took a minute longer to appreciate Lonnie than Blind Lemon. Lonnie was definitely a bluesman, but he took a left turn where Blind Lemon went right. Where Blind Lemon was raw, Lonnie was gentle. Lonnie was more sophisticated. His voice was lighter and sweeter, more romantic, I'd say. He had a dreamy quality to his singing and a lyrical way with the guitar. Unlike Blind Lemon, Lonnie sang a wide variety of songs. I liked that. I guess he found the strict blues form too tight. He wanted to expand. When he sang "Tomorrow Night," probably his most famous ballad, I understood that he was going to a place beyond the blues that, at the same time, never left the blues. Later I'd learn that Lonnie performed with Louis Armstrong and Duke Ellington. As my life went on and my passion for blues grew, it hurt me to see that Lonnie never got the critical acknowledgment he deserved. The scholars loved to praise the "pure" blues artists or the ones, like Robert Johnson, who died young and represented tragedy. It angers me how scholars associate the blues strictly with tragedy.

As a little kid, blues meant hope, excitement, pure emotion. Blues were about feelings. They seemed to bring out the feelings of the artist and they brought out my feelings as a kid. They made me wanna move, or sing, or pick up Reverend's guitar and figure out how to make those wonderful sounds. Blind Lemon and Lonnie hit me hardest, I believe, because their voices were so distinct, natural, and believable. I heard them talking to me. As guitarists, they weren't fancy. Their guitars were hooked up to their feelings, just like their voices.

Scholars also like to talk about the Delta bluesmen and how they influenced each other. They break down the blues, according to different parts of Mississippi and say each region gave birth to a style. Well, as a Delta boy, I'm here to testify that my two biggest idols—guys I flat-out tried to copy—came a long way from Mississippi. Blind Lemon was from Dallas and Lonnie from Louisiana. I later learned about Delta bluesmen like Robert Johnson and Elmore James and Muddy Waters. I liked them all, but no one molded my musical manner like Blind Lemon and Lonnie. They entered my soul and stayed. Sixty-five years after hearing them on Aunt Mima's precious Victrola, hardly a day goes by that I don't listen to them. When Lonnie sings from "Bow Legged Baby," "she's got big bow legs, wears her dress above her knees," I'm laughing like a little kid discovering blues for the first time.

But the discoveries at Aunt Mima's entailed more than the blues. There was Bessie Smith and Mamie Smith and Ma Rainey, to be sure, blues ladies who tore off the top of my head. I still hear songs like "Empty Bed Blues" and "Crazy Blues" and "See See Rider Blues." Mima also loved gospel. Among her collection of forty or fifty records were things by J. M. Reverend Gates, who sang songs like "Death's Black Train." There were jazz bands like Duke Ellington's, whose rhythms, more complicated than the beat of the blues, still fired my blood. Mima also had Jimmie Rodgers, a yodeler who happened to be white but who sang songs like "Blues, How Do You Do?" They called him the Singing Brakeman and I sang along with him.

Not all my musical impressions were made by Aunt Mima's records. At a tender age, I was fortunate enough to get next to a true-life bluesman. I'm talkin' 'bout Bukka White, my mother's first cousin.

Booker T. Washington White was the real deal. He had cut phono-
graph records for Victor and Vocalion with his name printed on the
label, and he lived in a glamorous place called Memphis, Tennessee.
He'd come to visit my mom and her family a couple of times a year:
midsummer and Christmas. He knew how plantation owners hate for
strangers to come 'round when the workers are busy, so he'd pick the
off-times and show up looking like a million bucks. Razor-sharp. Big
hat, clean shirt, pressed pants, shiny shoes. He smelled of the big city
and glamorous times; he looked confident and talked about things
outside our little life in the hills. He was a big-boned man, big head,
big fists, big arms, flashy teeth, and a beautiful smile when you looked
him in the eyes. He always had a good word and candy for the kids,
a real happy-go-lucky guy, joking and stroking everyone with com-
pliments and charm. He lit up my world. He could have been a con
man because you believed every word he said, but he wasn't; he was a
bluesman. I knew that because of the guitar he carried. His guitar was
as much a part of his person as his fancy big-city clothes.

He'd saw off a short piece of pipe just big enough to slip his fat
finger inside. Or sometimes he'd use a bottleneck, maneuvering that
sucker in his left hand, sliding up down up the strings. Man, you talk
about the prettiest sound this side of heaven! His vibrato gave me
goose bumps. Cousin Bukka was king of the slide guitar and a spine-
tingling storyteller whose songs like "Aberdeen Mississippi Blues"—
he came from Aberdeen—and "Shake 'em on Down" were popular
with people all over. He'd talk about playing roadhouses in Tennessee,
Arkansas, and Georgia where people gambled the night away. He had
to explain to me what gambling was. For a while, he'd lived in Chicago
with tall buildings and railroad trains running right through the city.
It was like hearing a fairy tale; it was too much for a little country boy
to understand.

Elizabeth H. Aydelott

Elizabeth H. Aydelott was born in 1921 in Poplarville where she began her lifetime commitment to volunteerism. No matter where she lived, "Libby" Aydelott was active in the basic four: her church, her children's schools, an active woman's club, and Scouting. She has volunteered with the Mississippi Historical Society, Friends of Mississippi Libraries, Family Research Association, Jackson Review Club, Mississippi Historical Trust, American Association of University Women, MUW Alumni Association, Arts Council of Clinton, Inc., Clinton Historical and Genealogical Society, Main Street Clinton, DAR, and UDC.

As I think back on my childhood, it is not hard to recognize the influence of my family and my town and to reflect on the drawbacks as well as the opportunities of this particular period of time.

There is a striking contrast between the 1920s and '30s of my own youth and the 1980s and '90s of the similar years of my grandchildren. I decided I am fortunate to have lived in my time and they are equally fortunate to have lived in their time.

For years I have had the firm feeling that the parents of my youth were especially strong, caring, and resourceful during a difficult period. Maybe it was just my particular situation to have been born in a very small town whose citizens handled their problems without burdening their children, but somehow managed to bring the whole family together to work out the crisis among themselves.

I am aware now, however, that there were those in our town who faced particular hardships and inequities. At this time, there was no integration of the races in this area. The families I associated with at home, in church, and at school did not represent all the residents of the area. It was, however, the environment in which I lived at that time.

I grew up in Poplarville in Pearl River County. My father, who was a native of Choctaw County, met my mother in her native Noxubee County. He was a graduate of Mississippi Agricultural and Mechanical College (A&M), now Mississippi State University, and she had finished a short period of time at Mississippi State Teachers College (now University of Southern Mississippi). He was the principal and she was a primary teacher at a small rural school. He used to laugh and say she was so puzzled about what to do with first-, second-, and third-grade pupils in one room for instruction in reading, writing, and arithmetic that she gave up teaching forever. Anyway, that's when they became engaged.

World War I began and my father was in the army. Mama said her father absolutely forbade her to marry Daddy until he came home from the army safe and sound. However, she did tell me that they had decided to marry when he finished his training in Arkansas, but he was given no leave and immediately shipped out.

When he returned from France he taught at the agricultural high school in Poplarville. At the end of the school year my parents were married, and they lived in an apartment in a dormitory at the high school. The next June, I was born in my grandfather's house in Macon. In the early twenties, very few small Mississippi towns had hospitals. Three and a half years later my brother was born in a small hospital in Poplarville. By this time my father was the principal of the Pearl River County Agricultural High School, a position he kept until I graduated from high school.

I have a distinct memory of being five years old and ready for primer. If you waited until you were six, when school was compulsory, you went to first grade. Our family moved to a house close enough for me to walk to school. Our street had the school in the middle, with a church on either side and houses on each end.

The first publicly supported junior college in Mississippi was established in Poplarville early in the twenties and was situated on the campus of the Pearl River County Agricultural High School, which already had dormitories and a dining facility. Additional buildings were added to accommodate the freshmen and sophomore college classes.

When I was about seven, our family moved to an apartment on the first floor of the boys' dormitory. I was puzzled by this but never asked why. I found out many years later that times were changing. My father's salary had been cut almost in half. I was also puzzled about why he walked the floor if the bank statement was late in the mail. I learned that he was sending money to my grandparents on the farm for their taxes. And years later I learned that he borrowed money on his insurance policy to avoid cashing the warrants issued in lieu of salary at a discount.

The Depression had begun toward the end of the first decade for us and ended at the close of the next decade with the beginning of World War II. The Depression was no picnic but, in our town, working together and sharing what we had made life bearable for most of us. That generation of adults worked out solutions to problems that are automatically done today by government agencies. At that time, solutions were found through friendship, kinship, or just a recognition of being able to do something easily and well for another human being who would do the same thing for you when the opportunity presented itself.

I think all of my friends realized, as I did, that times were hard. We got Christmas presents and a birthday present, but anything else was a great surprise. We wore hand-me-downs. Since women's dresses were shorter then, my mother took skirts from some of her old dresses and made clothes for me. I remember a time when I was about ten that for some reason I wanted high-top tennis shoes so badly. In my family your school shoes lasted for the whole school year. Finally, after much discussion, my mother reluctantly let me get them and I was delighted. Close to the end of the school year, I was to have a part in a program at the school for all parents and friends. I remember my mother, almost in tears, saying for me to please tell the teacher she was so sorry I didn't have better shoes. My Sunday shoes were too small by this time. It certainly didn't bother me to wear high-top tennis shoes to the program, but I was sorry my mother was so concerned that she couldn't afford to buy me more school shoes in May when I would just go barefoot most of the summer.

The college campus, as we called it, was a wonderful place for my brother and me. I failed to see it from my parents' viewpoint. My father had night responsibilities in the dormitory in addition to his daytime duties at school. My mother had a much smaller place to live. We ate in the dining hall at first but that was difficult with children three times a day and expensive, too. So, one room of our apartment became a dining facility with the addition of a bed for my brother. There were pecans to pick up on the campus. My mother kept some for our family and had the two of us take the rest to teachers living in the other dormitories. Students who brought a car to school sometimes would give us a ride around the campus in a rumble seat, which was an exciting treat for us. There was a chinaberry tree I would climb up in to read a book. The college library was available to me, and I could talk with and demonstrate to the librarian that I *was* able to understand the books I wanted to check out. My mother finally told her that nothing between the covers of a book would harm me. She also sent me on Fridays after school to borrow magazines, which the librarian loaned my mother for weekend reading.

Since the college was some distance from our school, my brother and I rode a school bus. The first one was some sort of a cab pulling a trailer with two long parallel benches and canvas sides. It was replaced later with a real bus.

My mother always subscribed to the *Macon Beacon* weekly newspaper. Every Monday after school I took the latest copy across the street to the experiment station and read it to an older lady who was blind. She told me so many stories about the people in the paper, some of whom she identified as either her cousins or mine. She was a lovely lady, originally from Macon, who had known my mother when she was a child. She told me so much about her life when she was young and taught me songs and games of that day. It was a pleasant way to learn the history of people and places connected with my family.

As the children in our town grew older, our parents involved us in all their activities. In small towns like ours most of the organizations were church, veteran, or school related. Our church was very small and was a combination of Presbyterians and Episcopalians. We had a Presbyterian minister one Sunday a month. After Sunday school on the other Sundays my family went to one of the two other churches in town with equal attendance at each. One Sunday night a month, for a few years, we had an Episcopal priest from Bay St. Louis for a service in our church. He became the bishop of Louisiana and that ended that. At first I went on Sunday afternoon to a youth group meeting at one church. When I was in high school I attended the Sunday night services with young people at the other church.

The ladies' auxiliary of one small church provided spring and fall clothing for a girl in the Palmer Orphanage in Columbus. I was her age and size. Winter and summer I made two trips from house to house, first to be measured, and afterwards to try on the clothes the ladies made. I kept that job a long time. Much later, when I was at the "W," which was at that time the Mississippi State College for Women, I was privileged to meet this girl in one of my classes.

My father was active in the American Legion and the Veterans of Foreign Wars. I remember an organization they formed for the daughters of veterans in our town. We were asked to pass out the little red poppies that represented Flanders Fields in France. People gave us donations to be used by the adult organization. We had white dresses with red, white, and blue bias tape at the neck and sleeves. We were assigned something to do at their barbecues and fish fries. On special holidays or civic occasions, grammar school students marched down Main Street to the courthouse. Some of us had poems to read and we usually sang an appropriate song. At school we had YWCA and YMCA groups in the upper grades where we did projects for the school. The PTA also used us when they needed our help.

I was a member of a Lone Star Troop of Girl Scouts when I was twelve. There was a group of mothers who formed a committee, found a leader, and connected us with the Girl Scouts of the USA. This was before we "got under the green umbrella" with councils in every state in the union. This is still a very important part of my life. I have been in six councils in five states, including Mississippi again at the present time. In the early sixties Girl Scouts of the USA helped me to learn how to work easily with all races while leading training courses with adults and leading troops with girls.

The American Legion in our town decided, for some reason, that we needed a drum and bugle corps. They bought us instruments and the band director at the college taught us to play and march, so we were part of every parade in town after that. A very special opportunity was worked out for us. We were carried by automobile to Bogalusa, where we caught the Rebel train to Jackson, toured the city, and were the last unit in the inauguration parade for the first term of Governor Hugh White.

The United Daughters of the Confederacy celebration of Memorial Day was a special treat for older children. We dressed in period costumes and danced the minuet.

There were two extra programs offered to us with a charge attached. One that I really enjoyed was "Expression" with a wonderful teacher whose income was completely provided by her pupils in the community. Those of us who took it had a weekly class at school. She taught us how to speak in public, alone or with others. My mother insisted that I take this class in third grade so I would be more comfortable than she had been when she was young and was required to participate in any oral presentation. After one year I no longer had lessons, but Miss Frankie used all her former students in plays she produced about twice a year, and which everyone in town always attended. All our mothers insisted that we participate. This was another example of an easy way to furnish an income for the teacher and to advertise to others what she could accomplish with children, and the memorizing and acting were of benefit to us. My mother always said you help people who need you and it always rewards you in some way.

Another amusing thing that frequently happened in this regard was that the United Daughters of the Confederacy was very important to this teacher and we often took advantage of that. At play practice someone would often wink at the rest of us and then make a reference to "Yankees," either favorable or not. Suddenly we'd have a respite in play practice and be treated to an emotional recitation about "our side" of that "invasion of our land." I wonder now if she didn't know what we were doing and was taking advantage of the opportunity to relate to us the history that she felt we should know. Her father was a Confederate veteran. You cannot imagine how this amused us, and nobody ever told a mother about it.

The other opportunity was music lessons. My teacher worked hard with me. Since I lived in an apartment, we no longer had a piano, so I had permission to practice during a study hall period at her house, one block from the school, on the three days she taught in Hattiesburg in the middle of the week. I played a little, then I read my book. A family member in an adjoining apartment told my mother to "tell Elizabeth to quit plinking the piano and read her book quietly."

Very occasionally, when I was in high school, I was asked to play the pump organ in a small church for Sunday school. I was now attending a Sunday night youth group at another church and loved the lively hymns they sang at night. I found a few in one hymnal and played them the next time. My father said, "Don't play those fast hymns because we don't know them." The next week, at whose request I never knew, my teacher marched me down to my church and saw to it that I could play three hymns she picked out, and she instructed me to play them if I was ever asked to play again.

During my high school years I kept a low profile. It was not easy to be the principal's daughter, as we did not have all the privileges of the college students on the same campus. Then there came a period of time when the public school system was changed in such a way that many teachers were affected. The primer (the year before first grade) was discontinued and the teacher requirements in education courses were increased. Two sisters who had taught these two classes for all of us in school were, of course, eliminated from the faculty. However, our parents handled that situation beautifully. The two sisters were encouraged to start a kindergarten in their home, which provided an income for them. It worked satisfactorily; after all, they had begun the education process for all of us. This was yet another example of the town taking care of its own in a beneficial way.

During my college years, 1938–1942, we were very aware of the fact that during the Depression a college degree would not give the assurance of a job in your field upon graduation. I had a major in secretarial science, a minor in my true love, history and social studies, and all my electives in education courses in case I had to teach, which I was not interested in at all.

December 7, 1941, changed all our lives forever. Suddenly there was a job for everybody. The boys were going to war and women were eligible for many jobs not available to us before; even the armed forces opened up jobs to us other than as nurses and secretaries. While the war changed the circumstances of my life, it could not and did not change the community values that my parents, my teachers, and the town of Poplarville had instilled in me.

I have always felt that I have been lucky in my life. The fact is that I did have the freedom to do the things I wanted to do and cared about. Looking back as I write this review, I am very thankful for what it has been my privilege to experience.

Robert C. Khayat

Robert C. Khayat was born in Moss Point in 1938, the third child of Eddie and Eva Khayat. A graduate of Moss Point High in 1956 and the University of Mississippi in 1961, he later received law degrees from Ole Miss in 1966 and Yale University in 1981. He played on championship Ole Miss football and baseball teams and spent four years with the NFL Washington Redskins. In 1995 he was named fifteenth chancellor of the University of Mississippi. He and his wife Margaret Denton Khayat have been married since 1962 and have two children and two grandchildren.

T he name of the town is Moss Point—a sleepy enclave located two miles inland on the Mississippi Gulf Coast. Situated at the confluence of the Pascagoula and Escatawpa rivers, laced with winding, marsh-lined bayous, the small community provided a safe haven for its 1,500 midcentury inhabitants. It also produced a disproportionate number of characters whose antics, activities, personalities, and peculiarities are indelibly etched in the memories of those of us, who, by virtue of the random nature of birthplace, had the good fortune of spending our childhood years there.

Established early in the nineteenth century as a port and staging area for international shipment of the abundant lumber supply of south Mississippi, the town had had its foundations laid by cosmopolitan people who understood and valued beauty, grace, and charm. Taking full advantage of the enticing climate and the natural beauty of the area, the founders and early settlers created a planned community—things were where they were supposed to be.

Neatly laid out streets were lined with live oaks and enhanced by grand homes; those oaks were draped with wiry Spanish moss, and together, with the bluff overlooking the juncture of the rivers, inspired the name Moss Point.

Persons unfamiliar with the town may find the name quaint or romantic—perhaps fictional sounding. For residents of the community, however, Moss Point has a unique personality, a spirit, and a soul. The town is an essential part of who we are.

Growing up in Moss Point during the years between the Great Depression and the turbulent '60s was an idyllic experience. Simplicity of life, close personal relationships developed without regard to race, religion, financial status, or political preference; security of person and property; and a unique familiarity between adults and children produced an uncommon and, now, almost forgotten lifestyle.

The following vignette is my attempt to preserve a bit of the unique spirit of one small town. If this effort is offensive to anyone or if it is in any way inaccurate, I apologize to those persons and to the town. The place and the people are warmly and affectionately remembered.

Although I don't want to hear her say it and I am unrealistically hoping she will forget, I know the time has come: "It's 2:15, Robert; come wash your face and hands. Get your books or you'll be late for your lesson."

Late for my lesson! I'd rather take a strong dose of Milk of Magnesia than go to that piano lesson. Requiring a ten-year-old boy to spend thirty minutes of a July afternoon in the company of an elderly lady in front of a dark, old upright piano borders on cruel and unusual punishment, or so it seemed at the time.

Knowing that I had to leave the afternoon activity of baseball or fishing or playing in the woods with my friends to go to the lesson led to the suggestion that I should run away from home. Devious attempts to avoid the misery, transparent and obvious though they were, became a part of the weekly ritual. Stomachaches, sore fingers, lost books, and possibility of rain were unpersuasively offered as compelling reasons to cancel the appointment, but to no avail—I had to go.

Recognizing that continued excuses were having little effect, I dutifully began preparation for the anguish and torment. Hurried swipes of a cold, damp washcloth (without soap) constituted my youthful attempt at physical hygiene. Efforts to select the wrong books or forget one or more of the necessary but objectionable scores (such as "Song of the Volga Boatmen") were thwarted by the knowing, watchful eye of my mother. Statements that my bicycle was broken were discounted or rejected outright. Finally, threats of a spanking "when your daddy gets home" made it abundantly clear that I had to go to the lesson.

Mounting the bicycle with the books clutched under my arm, I would set out for my destination feeling much abused. As I proceeded from our yard and into the street, familiar landmarks presented possible opportunities for delay or even abortion of the mission. With half an hour allotted for the lesson, every minute was precious; if lucky, I might be delayed by the big boys at the store, or perhaps by an accident at the bayou bridge.

The first checkpoint along the one-and-one-half-mile route was Couch's store. For some reason unknown to me then (and now), the small porch and rough wooden benches at the front of the store held an attraction teenage boys could not resist. Clearly, they were not lured there by the limited assortment of goods offered for sale in the store, nor was comfort an overriding consideration on the part of the carpenter who built the crude benches for the porch. Memories of the site invariably include half a dozen "big boys" loitering on the porch—whittling, having lukewarm soft drinks, chewing tobacco or, perhaps, smoking cigarettes. Occasionally, one would have a guitar and would be singing risqué songs such as "Flaming Mammy" or "The Woodpecker Song," to the delight of his small but enthusiastic audience. You could immediately detect when an off-color joke or song was in progress by the way they gathered in a huddle around the boy who had the floor.

Perhaps the most popular activity of the group (known by insiders as the Dirty Dozen although there were no more than six or eight of them) was harassment of the passersby. For women walking to work, this could mean having mild obscenities shouted at them; for younger boys, it could mean various forms of hazing such as twisting of fingers or pulling "frogs" in their arms. For a ten-year-old en route to an unwanted piano lesson, it could mean an alternate form of torture, unpleasant perhaps, but preferred to thirty minutes in front of a piano.

Approaching the store and the possible interruption of my journey produced a mixture of fear and excitement. Unsure of how severe the harassment would be, I was somewhat apprehensive; on the other hand, it was possible that it would provide an acceptable excuse for missing all or part of the lesson. Usually the interruption would be brief—consisting only of a few comments such as "Where're you going, sissy—to play the piano?" or "Let's see your drawers, boy, do they have lace on them?"

Standing out in my memory, however, is a comment made by one of the regulars known as "Ring." I recall the day he stopped me and to my surprise said, "Don't pay any mind to them. I wish I knew how to play a piano." Paradoxical behavior for someone who enjoyed being perceived as "tough"—but the brief exchange made a lasting impression on me.

Thinking back, I suppose the attraction of the store had something to do with peer acceptance and a twisted form of coming of age. Although I never became a regular in the group that gathered on the porch, I came to accept their presence and learned to tolerate their minor intrusions into my life.

Proceeding toward my destination, having failed to be justifiably detained at the store, I knew that the small wooden bridge at the bayou provided a second possible obstacle to the misery that awaited me at the home of the piano teacher. The bayou was an important landmark in our town, having political and social meaning as well as geographic significance. The dark, narrow body of water was approximately seventy-five feet wide but was bordered on either side by marsh which extended some two hundred feet to the high ground. Raw sewage emptied into the bayou—a fact which many found abhorrent but which, to the delight of the Dirty Dozen, served as a basis for selection of an appropriate name for the bayou. In addition to providing a harbor for small houseboats and a fishing hole for those willing to eat the fish caught there, the bayou was a neighborhood division point. All territory east of the bayou was known as "town" since the tiny cluster of shops which served the community's commercial needs were located in that area; the neighborhood west of the bayou was primarily residential and was referred to as "bayou." Group or team affiliation was determined by the bayou; if you lived on the west side, you were "bayou," on the east you were "town."

A wooden bridge, built many years before, spanned the water, adequately serving the needs of vehicular traffic, little as there was. The presence of the marsh necessitated construction of an elevated walkway which reached from high ground to high ground, being some three hundred feet in length. Approximately four feet wide, the wooden walkway was rendered reasonably safe by the presence of a handrail, perpendicular to the walk, resembling a corral or loading chute for livestock. The handrail prevented pedestrians from carelessly stepping off the walkway into the bayou, although the eighteen-inch spaces between the horizontal boards naturally induced youthful users of the bridge to hang their legs through, throw rocks into the bayou, and even attempt a high-wire act.

The rail was also a convenient leaning post for my bicycle as I paused on the bridge to ponder my fate. In fact, my calculations indicated that if I sat on my bike, leaning against the rail, there was a good chance that my music books would fall out of my hands and into the bayou some ten feet below. I envisioned the disappointment of a modern-day Robinson Crusoe, excitedly lifting the paper from his beach, only to discover my music books!

Although we occasionally experienced hurricanes of sufficient force to dislodge music books from the loose grasp of an unwilling holder, those winds refused to present themselves when I needed them. My stay on the bridge would end in mild disappointment and awareness that nothing short of death would spare me from that lesson.

Approaching the small green frame house where she lived and taught, I often wondered why she did it. Why would anyone in her right mind spend her afternoons inside with a piano and a ten-year-old prisoner? Aware that she lived there with her daughter, I was never sure what had become of her husband. Was he dead or had he abandoned her? In my mind, I assumed he simply walked away, because I was sure that, had he stayed, he would have died from overexposure to the ascending and descending notes produced by unskilled fingers on the slightly out-of-tune piano.

I later learned that she did it for the money, which she desperately needed. Although I don't recall having good feelings about the lessons, I do remember that she commanded respect and admiration from her unwilling pupils. She must have been in her midfifties when I came to know her but she seemed much older. As soft and quiet as the smooth pastel blouses she wore, she had remarkable patience. And she smelled good. She was one of those people who always gave the appearance of having just bathed, powdered, and brushed. Her dark, slightly graying hair was held neatly in place by small combs on each side of her head, framing her pretty face, interrupted only by the small wire glasses she wore. Her hands were small and her fingers nimble. In the shadows of her living room where the lesson was conducted, her hands appeared to be translucent. It seemed that she had never been exposed to the sun.

In addition to the dark, upright piano and bench, the room was sparingly furnished with Victorian pieces, including a small love seat, rocker, one side chair, and several small oak tables. On each table was an embroidered lace doily, slightly yellowed from many years of use. The lighting in the room was poor. But for the fragrance of lilacs emanating from her body and the hint of perfume always present in her handkerchief, the room would have been a musty place.

The lesson began with a confession by the pupil that, no, he had not practiced thirty minutes a day since the last lesson. Hoping against hope that the rationalization offered would mitigate her dissatisfaction with the anticipated response, I would enthusiastically and un-

persuasively present my excuses. For a few minutes she would patient-
ly and quietly explain that all the truly great pianists were men; that
to be good required practice; and that if I refused to practice, I would
never learn to play. The lecture was followed by unskilled attempts to
work through the awkward, unfamiliar tunes she had selected for the
week.

Watching the minute hand on the small, cream-colored Westclox
clock resting on top of the piano crawl slowly toward the thirty-min-
ute mark while keeping my eye on the score was difficult. Somehow,
we would get through the lesson, she would faithfully make assignments for the next week, I'd hand her fifty cents, and she'd offer
lemonade, which I hardly ever accepted. All I wanted was out! With
strains of "Be sure to practice" and "See you next Wednesday" ringing in my ears, I rushed out of the house without speaking to the next
pupil seated uneasily in the wicker chair on the front porch.

Exhilaration flooded my soul as my foot hit the sidewalk and my
hands touched the chrome handlebars of my bicycle. Free at last—
back to the ballgame—no music for seven days!

I wondered at the time why my parents insisted that I take piano
lessons. I saw little value in the experience, and, even when I envisioned myself as the next Chopin, I could generate no interest in the
activity. After nearly three years, my parents conceded defeat and the
lessons ended. Thereafter my afternoons were spent on the lake, in
the woods, or in a game of ball. Not until I had become an adult did
I realize the personal loss sustained by my failing to continue the lessons.

Although I missed my opportunity to become a pianist, fond
memories dominate my thoughts regarding those lessons. Foremost
is the quiet courage of the teacher who found a way not only to survive adversity with dignity but, in fact, to assume an important role
in the lives of her pupils and in the community at large. The lessons
taught by great teachers include values reflected in their lives—courage, honesty, respect, integrity, sensitivity—and those are the lessons I
learned in front of that old piano.

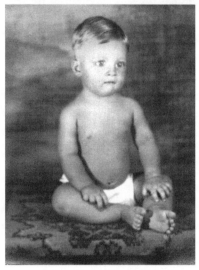

Donald H. Peterson

Donald H. Peterson, born in Winona in 1933, is a graduate of the United States Military Academy at West Point. He received his master's degree in nuclear engineering from the Air Force Institute of Technology. As a test pilot for the U.S. Air Force he logged 5,300 flying hours. In 1983 as a NASA astronaut mission specialist on the *Challenger* he spent four hours and fifteen minutes in extra vehicular activity (space walk). He has logged 120 hours in space. Peterson dedicates the following essay to the memory of Mrs. M. L. Branch, a dedicated, gifted teacher and a wonderful friend.

For the first seventeen years of my life I lived less than a half mile from a place we kids called Spooky Canyon. To get there I just walked west on Summit Street up "cemetery hill" and followed the dirt-gravel road a couple of hundred yards around the west side of the cemetery. And there, just off the right side of the road, was a whole different world for a young boy.

Of course, it wasn't really a canyon; it was about an acre of interlinked red-walled gullies with white sand floors that sliced down to a depth of eight or maybe ten feet through the surface of weeds and grass and wildflowers and scrub oaks and pines that made up the surrounding terrain. And I never really felt scared of the place, so I guess it wasn't truly spooky either.

But it held a kind of magic for an eight-year-old boy—a place where you weren't bound by reality. Within that acre I was Buck Jones with my six-shooter riding hard through Death Valley in pursuit of rustlers; or Tarzan with my fearsome knife protecting Jane and the creatures of my escarpment from greedy hunters; or Space Ranger (there was a character called Space Ranger in a dime comic book in those days) with my disintegrator pistol battling alien monsters on Mars; or Robin Hood leading my band of outlaws against the evil sheriff of Nottingham. The hills and gullies and sand and trees of Spooky Canyon could become any place my imagination wanted.

Usually I was alone there, but it wasn't a lonely place. It was filled with the sights and sounds of scampering squirrels and lizards, the hum of insects, the calls of songbirds, the glitter of sunlight filtered through leaves, the sound of wind in the trees, and the thousand shapes of wind-sculpted clouds moving silently across the untroubled sky of childhood.

As I grew older I still loved to go there, maybe out of nostalgia or maybe to enjoy a different kind of magic. It was not an awesome setting, but I have lots of lifelong memories of the hours I spent there. In my mind I can still see the flash of lightning and hear the rumble of thunder from an approaching summer storm, and the memory of getting soaked in a cooling shower on a blistering hot afternoon still makes me smile. Few things in my life have seemed more beautiful than the rays of a late afternoon autumn sun slanting through multicolored leaves, turning the red clay gullies even redder and making the white sand look pink. And once on a chilly winter afternoon under a cold gray sky I spent an hour there just to look at the place under the cover of a light snowfall, quiet and somber, as if it were resting before the new burst of life that spring would bring.

The magic of Spooky Canyon never died for me, but I left Winona three months before my eighteenth birthday in 1951, and my visits over the years since then have been brief and focused on family. So, I visited Spooky Canyon only one time in the last fifty years. In the mid-to-late sixties, I took my two oldest children there to show them my favorite childhood haunt. They were too young to really appreciate my feelings about the place, and it was an incredibly hot summer day, so we didn't stay very long. But at least they did see the place and enjoy romping around the gullies.

I did not know it at the time, but that would turn out to be the last time I saw Spooky Canyon. And I can never see it again, because it's not there anymore. Winona grew and needed a place to dump its garbage, and the empty gullies of Spooky Canyon met the need. And in a way it makes me sad to know that one of the places that made my young life happy is forever gone.

I never knew who owned that land, but I believe it was a man named Ferguson who had a sand and gravel business. There was a house on the road just north of Spooky Canyon and there were often dump trucks in the driveway, and I seem to remember there were signs on the trucks with Ferguson Sand and Gravel on them. But the sand and gravel must have come from some other place, because I don't remember anyone doing anything to change Spooky Canyon very much during the seventeen years I lived in Winona. I have often wondered if the owner left the place untouched for all those years just because so many of us enjoyed it so much. I never thanked him, but if he did that for us, I am grateful.

It's been more than a half century since those boyhood times, and I've seen and heard and done some things that were more impressive by adult standards, but none of them made me any happier than a day in Spooky Canyon.

Keith Tonkel

Keith Tonkel, born in 1936, grew up in Bay St. Louis and later studied for the ministry at Millsaps College and Emory University. He joined Wells United Methodist Church in Jackson as pastor in 1969. He became one of twenty-eight white Methodist ministers who publicly signed the "Born of Conviction" statement which denounced racism. He has remained at Wells for thirty-eight years, and during this time the church has grown in membership and ministries. He teaches Sunday School weekly on television and radio. He and his wife Pat have three children.

Relationships are made of relationships, not blood. When blood and positive and nourishing relationships come together, that is a very good thing.

Keith Sawer was my grandfather—"step-grandpa" if you let others define your realities. My mom's dad died a few months before she was born, so Keith Sawer was the only father she ever knew. He was a Britisher, an Oxford graduate and sometime teacher there, and in this country a businessman who owned a steamboat line that did worldwide trade until the height of the First World War. I was named for my dad, Dennie, and my grandfather, Keith.

Grandpa's marriage to my complex grandmother did not work out, so Mom had him come to live with us. We got to know him even better when his business was bad, and after he had been diagnosed with extensive cancer of the stomach.

Our place in New Orleans was a duplex on Ringold Street in Lakeview. It was a double-story house with two bedrooms upstairs and a kitchen, bath, and living room down. Grandpa stayed in one of the bedrooms, Mom and Dad in the other. I had a place on the back porch next to the hot water heater. There was a small dairy across the street, and the nearest grocery store, a "mom and pop" kind, was a good four blocks away. Mr. Mullotouf and his family owned the store.

Grandpa was not well at all. In fact, the cancer was such that he had to wear large gauze pads on his stomach all the time. In health, he had been a very large man, tall and full bodied, not heavy, but well built. Now, he was thin, gray, and weaker than he would admit.

One Saturday morning he said to me as I brought coffee and toast to his room: "Would you like to go to the grocery store with me this morning? I'll buy you a treat."

"Why do you need to go to the store?" I responded. "I'll go for you if there is something you have to have."

"No," he said with that gentle smile of his. "I owe Mr. Mullotouf some money, and I want to pay him."

"I'll take care of that too," I said. "I'd be glad to pay him for you."

"But Keith"—he spoke softly but with conviction—"you don't owe the money. I do. Can you take time to walk with me?"

It took a long time to dress and an equally long time to walk the four blocks to the store. Grandpa would stop for a breath, tap me on the chin with his cane and say: "Don't walk pigeon-toed, son. Keep those feet spread out." I had some kind of congenital twist in my gait, and was indeed pigeon-toed. Then we would move on a bit until we finally came to the corner store.

I was amazed when Grandpa pulled coins from his pocket and paid Mr. Mullotouf three cents. "I think that makes us even, doesn't it, Bernard?" Grandpa said to the store owner.

"Now, Keith, you know I didn't want you to pay that balance. It's too small to worry about."

"It's obligation, not size that matters, Mr. Mullotouf, and you work hard for your living. I am glad to be one of your customers."

Integrity is a learned response.

A few years later, we moved to Bay St. Louis from New Orleans for my sister's health. My sister, Denise, was born with lung problems and asthma. We would take turns walking her during the night, since she never slept the whole night through.

One weekend on a visit to "the Bay," as we called it, we awoke one morning with a definite scare. Denise had slept all night long. Mom, in fact, thought that she was probably dead. You can imagine our relief when we found her sound asleep in the small crib we had brought with us in the car. We all moved to Bay St. Louis that same month.

By now Grandpa's illness was far worse. Mom would often say, "They only gave him a few months to live, and it's been more than seven years now."

Grandpa and my dad's mom, Momsie, had become quite close friends. I remember distinctly Grandpa Keith talking to Momsie about Plato while she sat in his room with a piece of sewing. Momsie did not have a day of formal education, and did not have the slightest idea who Plato was, but she was such a committed listener that Grandpa said, "My, my, what an intelligent and lovely lady."

That evening, Momsie said to Mom and me, "I don't think Mr. Sawer is very well. I feel that he may not be with us for much longer." Mom and I passed that off without much thought. Grandpa was supposed to have gone on long before now.

But the next morning, he was weak and hurting. "Keith," he called out to me from his room. "Yes, sir," I answered. "Can you help me up?" he asked when I appeared at his door. "I want to bathe and change my pajamas, and a few more things." I said, "It's Saturday, and I've got time."

Shortly, he was bathed and in clean bedclothes. It was very difficult getting him back into the bed, but when we accomplished that, he said: "Would you please get me my Bible." He was a devout Anglican. I brought the Bible. He was holding his right hand hard against his stomach. You could see pain on his face. "If you don't mind, open it to Psalm 27," he said. I did so, and offered the book to him. "Read me the first two lines, please." I found the place and read: "The Lord is my light and my salvation, whom shall I fear? The Lord is the strength of my life, of whom shall I be afraid?" "Yes," he said with emphasis, "that's the one. Now help me put the open book gently over the bandages on my stomach, if you will." I did so. "And now, son, would it be asking too much for you to go and close the venetian blinds for me?" I did that, too.

"One more thing, please go and tell your dear mama that I send to her my best thanks and deepest love. It's time for me to go home."

I knew this was something serious, and so I literally ran to the kitchen for Mom. When we came back, he was gone. Home.

He was, we had always heard, a Knight of the Garter in the Cabinet of King George VI, and was thus buried weeks later with Royal Honors. I was eleven years old and unable to attend because I developed a ruptured appendix and had surgery soon after Grandpa died, but they said the service was very special. He had a purple sash across his chest and a gold medallion, and members of the Queen's Guard assisted.

When they told me, I was glad. He was such a wealthy man in so many ways. He deserved something nice. Grandpa died with thirty-six cents to his name. He left it to me.

I am as old now, perhaps a bit older than he was when he "went home." It took me a while to understand that integrity is learned. Virtue develops from example. Grandpa gave some of both to all he touched, and more besides.

When later I came to feel called to the ministry, my dad, a night-club entertainer, said to me, "My God, son, there's no future in that!" We all laughed. Our family sacrificed for me to attend Millsaps College and, later, Emory University. Most of the family was present for my graduation. It was made all the more special because I had been very ill for a long time, and was not expected to make it to seminary or ordination. But I had. I was fine, and thankful to God, and medicine, and the prayers of many. The only disappointment was that Grandpa wasn't there. Everybody but Grandpa.

Except that he was present. In the integrity I had learned, in the virtue he extended to all who really knew him. Grandpa was a great spirit—the kind that helps mold and direct lives. In that same spirit, he was there that evening. And as I write this, something of Grandpa, who never saw a computer, flows through fingers to keys, and all from the heart.

I'm proud to bear your name, Grandpa.

I asked him once if he knew the origin of our name, Keith. I had heard it meant "courageous," and once I read on a coffee mug that it meant "outdoorsman." Grandpa answered, "A keith is a windy place, my child. A kind of safe harbor where boats are protected as the wind blows over masts and sails." "Courageous" or "outdoorsman" would probably have been better for a preacher than "windy place," but integrity requires the truth, and wind has virtues of its own.

Samuel Jones

Samuel Jones, composer/conductor was born in Inverness in 1935 and received his B.A. from Millsaps College and his M.A. and Ph.D. in composition from the Eastman School of Music. He served as conductor of the Rochester Philharmonic, the Saginaw Symphony, and music advisor of the Flint Symphony. He founded the Alma Symphony and in 1973 established the Shepherd School of Music at Rice University. He lives in Seattle where he has served for over a decade as Composer in Residence of the Seattle Symphony Orchestra. He was inducted into the first class of Mississippi Musicians Hall of Fame and is a four-time winner of the Music Award of the Mississippi Institute of Arts and Letters. The following essay is based on his answers to questions posed by Joanna Smolko, a graduate student at the University of Pittsburgh, for her doctoral dissertation, an examination of composers' usage of shape-note hymns in the twentieth century.

My grandmother, Elizabeth Knight Jones (1882–1974), never realized, I am sure, that with the simple act of singing to her grandson she was planting a seed that would help to make a composer at the same time as she was giving him the idea for one of his most important compositions. This is a story of a young, musically inclined Mississippi boy and the old shaped-note hymns of the past.

The earliest contact with shaped-note notation that I can remember was seeing those "strange" sharply angled notes in hymnbooks. I grew up in Indianola, Mississippi (population 5,000, at that time), in the 1940s, and my family went to church in the Indianola First Baptist

Church. Most of the hymnals had regular notation, but quite a few shaped-note versions of the hymnals were peppered throughout the seat backs of the pews.

I suppose those shaped-note hymnals were available because some of the church members had moved to "town" from the surrounding rural areas, where the practice of singing from shaped-note music at all-day singings with dinner-on-the-ground was still commonplace on certain Sundays. As a young boy I remember being taken by my parents to some of those old singings. My father had grown up in "the country," the son of a well-regarded itinerant Baptist preacher and sharecropper. My dad liked to go back to his roots, and he also did it because he was by then involved in local county politics. He had worked himself through college. His family was dirt poor, and he was the first of his large family to pull himself out of the bondage of the almost-indentured servitude of the sharecropping system. Having recently been elected the superintendent of education of our county, Dad must have felt that connecting with the people at the singings was politically expedient as well as personally enjoyable.

As a young boy in the early grades of elementary school I had mixed feelings about the singings. Instead of the standard, mainline church hymns I was used to, there were these "strange" hymns with often irregular rhythms. And instead of a more cultivated vocal sound with what I regarded as a natural vibrato, everybody was singing with what sounded to me then like a hard, punched sound. To my young, inescapably prejudiced ears, I rather disliked it. I also remember that the texture was decidedly different. Only years later, after graduate school training as a composer, did I know why it sounded different.

I remember other, nonmusical things about the singings vividly, such as the abundant food—endless piles of fried chicken and incredible pies and cakes. And I remember the heat, and how folks fanned themselves with cardboard fans, which usually had advertising from a funeral home. And I still remember one of the funniest sights of my young childhood: an old gentleman in his shirtsleeves who was totally bald and who had a large comb sticking prominently up from his shirt pocket!

My grandparents (whom I often visited while they still lived on tenant farms, moving from one small farmhouse to another every two or three years) were regular attendees of the singings, and they knew and loved many of the old sacred harp hymns. One of my earliest memories of my grandmother was of her bouncing me as a very young boy on her knees and singing something in syllables I didn't understand. The tune, though, I remembered vividly, and some of the syllables: *So-la-fa . . . fa . . . fa-fa, la, so, fa, la . . . la . . . la-la.* I must have been three or four years old at the time. (That would have been around 1938 or '39, and my grandmother would have been in her midfifties.) Of course, I didn't know anything about the tune and never knew its name until years later (after my boyhood love for music had led me into my life's work as a composer and conductor) when I began working on what would turn out to be one of my most-performed compositions, *Let Us Now Praise Famous Men.*

Let Us Now Praise Famous Men was commissioned by the Shenandoah County Bicentennial Committee to commemorate the two-hundredth anniversary of that storied Virginia county. The piece was to be premiered on August 12, 1972. I was greatly honored, of course, and looked forward to the creative process of conceiving and composing the work. I was also extremely busy. By that time I had worked myself up from assistant conductor to full conductor of the Rochester Philharmonic and was conducting some eighty-five concerts per year. But this new composition would be a labor of great love, since I had had a close association with the Shenandoah Valley, where a conducting workshop (sponsored by the American Symphony Orchestra League) was located which I had attended and served as a teacher for years. Somehow I found the time to write the piece.

When I discovered that the Shenandoah Valley was important to the development and spread of the rural church singing school movement of the nineteenth century (it was both a publishing center, where many of the shaped-note hymnals were produced, and a dissemination center, where summer retreats and singing schools were held), this became important information for my new piece, as I could sense the strong possibility of some kind of orchestral fantasia based on these old hymns.

Almost immediately, as I was thinking about finding some of these old hymns, the tune my grandmother had bounced me to as a little boy came back to my consciousness. I sat down right then and quickly composed seven variations on that old tune, still unnamed in my mind but intensely vivid in my memory after some thirty-five years. Though I didn't quite know how it would ultimately be used, I sensed strongly that this was the start of my new piece.

I went to the library to do some research. I perused a number of the old shaped-note hymnals and read everything I could find on the subject, especially the writings of George Pullen Jackson. I found a number of old tunes that I considered as likely possibilities for melodic material for my new piece. And in the process I found my grandmother's tune! Its name was "Murillo's Lesson," and it was included in *The Sacred Harp* (p. 358). I had already composed my seven variations on the first half of the tune, the segment my grandmother had sung for me. I saved the second half for use later in my composition, to help close it out.

In the process of this research I discovered that these old tunes were much more interesting and sophisticated than my boyhood prejudices had allowed me to see. They were full of unusual rhythms and turns of phrase, and I could see that this material was a great resource for the contemporary composer. In addition to this, when I came across the Alan Lomax recordings of Sacred Harp Singings for the Library of Congress I gained a new appreciation for the sound of this style of singing. Instead of sounding strange, it seemed to me now sturdy, honest, unadorned, open, strong, rhythmically direct— all qualities which reflected the people of the soil from which this music (and my family and myself) had sprung.

As a postscript, let me add that in the late summer of that year

(1972), not too long before she died, we made a memorable family trip to visit my grandmother, during which I played for her a tape of the premiere performance. She was very frail then, but she found the energy to sit up and listen. When the music transitioned to the song she had sung to me, a great slow smile spread over her face. Her eyes lit up as of old, and she said, "That's 'Murillo's Lesson'!" That the notes of that melody would be returning to her, now in full orchestral and variational garb in a composition by her grandson, was almost too much to take in. It was one of the most touching moments of my life, being able to share it with her and thank her for the gift of her music.

Jim Weatherly

Jim Weatherly was born in 1943 and is a Ponotoc native. He was an All SEC quarter-back for the Ole Miss Rebels in 1964 before moving to Los Angles to pursue a career as a singer-songwriter. He wrote for and collaborated with Gladys Knight and the Pips on many top ten recordings. He had numerous other country, pop, R&B, jazz, and gospel hits. In 2001 the NEA and the Recording Industry of America placed his song "Midnight Train to Georgia" among the thirty "Songs of the Century." He was inducted into the Nashville Songwriters Hall of Fame and the Mississippi Musicians Hall of Fame. He lives in Brentwood, Tennessee, with his wife Cynthia and children Brighton and Zack.

Misty Mississippi Morning

Rows and rows of houses line the neatly laid out street
All the yards are silent cause the kids are still asleep
The streetlights all grow dimmer as the sun begins to streak
Across the haze
The six o'clock whistle tells the town it's time to rise
A distant passing train echoes faintly in reply
People stumble from their beds wiping sleep from their eyes
Still in a daze
 It's a misty Mississippi morning
 The dew is still hanging in the air
 Sunshine's dripping from the sky like honey
 There's not a cloud to be seen anywhere
 The breeze seems to blow straight from heaven

Scented with the honeysuckle vines
Those misty Mississippi mornings
Come back to me in pictures and rhymes
To linger soft as summer in my mind
Shadows touch down softly as they skip across the lawns
Playing hide and seek with the brand new silky dawn
And if you listen closely you can hear the day's first song
In the morning chimes
The harmony is sung by a peaceful meadowlark
As the picture comes to life, dogs begin to run and bark
While the old men sit and whittle on the benches in the park
Just killing time
It's a misty Mississippi morning
The dew is still hanging in the air
Sunshine's dripping from the sky like honey
There's not a cloud to be seen anywhere
The breeze seems to blow straight from heaven
Scented with the honeysuckle vines
Those misty Mississippi mornings
Come back to me in pictures and rhymes
To linger soft as summer in my mind.

Jim Weatherly, © *Universal Music, ASCAP*

It's never been more evident to me how things change with the passing of time. The world that I knew growing up in Mississippi only exists now in my memories and in my songs. What a wonderful world it was.

I grew up in Pontotoc, a small farming community located between Tupelo and Oxford on Highway 6 in northeast Mississippi. My mother, Edith, was a housewife (see, I told you times have changed) and my dad, Ike, was a lineman for the Pontotoc Power Association. I had a wonderful childhood. We weren't rich, but I didn't know it and I didn't care. We had family—a big family with aunts, uncles, cousins, and friends. I have two sisters, Sherrie and Elise, and one brother,

Shan, who all still live in Mississippi. On Sundays during the spring and summer, we would go over to my grandparents' house (Nanny and Daddy James) to spend the afternoon. The grown-ups would sit out under the huge oak tree in the northwest corner of the yard next to the big old house and talk. All of us kids and some of the grown-ups would play football and baseball and fly kites in the big green grassy yard. When shadows started to fall around dusk, we'd catch lightning bugs and put them in jars to make lanterns. Gradually everyone would drift into the house, and Mom and Dad, uncles Billy and Richard, and aunts Jean and Mary Ann gathered around the piano in the living room to sing hymns and gospel songs while another aunt, Billy's wife, Jane, played the piano. She was a great piano player and they were all really good singers. I used to love to listen to them and sometimes, even though I was little, I would join in. It was really a warm, happy time in my life.

I remember running through the woods on lazy summer days, and lying down on my back on a soft green bed of grass, looking up and watching the fluffy marshmallow clouds being pushed along by the southern breeze. I remember staying out after dark and playing Kick the Can and Capture the Flag and all sorts of games with my friends. It was a different time then, a gentler time, time to do everything, and time to do nothing but dream and listen to the radio. I soaked up the music of Elvis Presley, Ricky Nelson, Pat Boone, Brenda Lee, Connie Francis, the Chordettes, the Diamonds, and many more too numerous to name on WMPS out of Memphis. Late at night I'd lie in bed and tune in to WLAC out of Nashville on my little plastic radio where John R and Gene Nobles played all the great R&B acts like Ray Charles, the Cadillacs, Johnnie and Joe, Chuck Berry, Etta James, Muddy Waters, Howlin' Wolf, Bo Diddley, and Big Joe Turner. Those were the years in the early and mid-fifties when I really began to get into music.

I started out playing the ukulele because some of the guys around town had gotten them and were learning to play. The fad of the day, I guess.

One Christmas, I must have been around ten or eleven, I got my first guitar. It was a Silvertone hollow body. I was in high cotton, as we say in the South. I taught myself to play using the Mel Bay chord book that came with it. A year or so later, I saw a guitar in a catalog that I really wanted. It was a fine-looking guitar. It was a Harmony electric and was a cool, light copper color. My mother said she would help me pay for it if I mowed yards to earn some money. I worked my tail off, but I was finally able to get it. My dad made my first amplifier out of an old radio. He was an electrician so he knew how to do those things. It wasn't exactly high tech by today's standards, but it did the trick for a while. The next Christmas I begged for a new amplifier, but my dad told me it was too expensive. I was heartbroken. On Christmas morning, under the tree was the amp that I wanted. Santa had brought it. Wonderful memories, wonderful times.

Daddy James owned a small appliance store, Roberson Electric Supply, on a corner of the town square in Pontotoc. He had a little section in back where he sold records. He let me pick the records for him to buy on his monthly trip to the Pop Tunes Record Store in Memphis. When he got home he would give me the ones I wanted. I had them all: rockabilly, R&B, pop, country, all the hits of the day.

I grew up listening to and singing all kinds of music. The earliest were Sunday school songs and hymns that I learned in church. Then came the singing cowboys like Roy Rogers, Gene Autry, Jimmy Wakely, Tex Ritter, Eddie Dean. Nanny once told me that when I was three or four, I would sit out on the front steps of her house and make up cowboy songs. Then she laughed. That's where the songwriting started, I guess. In grammar school we sang a lot of old Stephen Foster songs like "Camptown Races," "Old Folks at Home," and "My Old Kentucky Home," as well as a lot of patriotic songs. Those songs had a big influence on me. I loved the simple, plaintive, down-home way that Stephen Foster wrote. My mother and my aunts liked the pop songs of Frank Sinatra, Perry Como, Eddie Fisher, Dean Martin, Frankie Laine, Rosemary Clooney, Doris Day, Patti Page, and Johnny Ray. I used to listen to these records at Nanny's house on the latest record player because Daddy James sold them in his appliance store. I was influenced a great deal in my writing by these great singers and early songs like "I'll Be Seeing You," "You Belong To Me," "Allegheny Moon."

My dad loved gospel music. In the mornings he'd get up before the rest of us while it was still dark outside and turn the radio on to a gospel music station. His favorites were the Statesmen Quartet and the Blackwood Brothers. My dad's dad (Daddy Deck) was somewhat of a gospel songwriter himself, and traveled with a gospel group on the weekends to sing in churches and all-night singings in the surrounding counties.

As you can see, I came from a very musical family. Elvis was heavily influenced by gospel music as well as I. A lot of my friends, mostly the older guys, were into country music. They turned me on to Hank Williams, Lefty Frizzell, Eddy Arnold, Webb Pierce, Ray Price, and many others. Hank Williams inspired many a songwriter with his songs about love and life, me included. I loved all kinds of music, but it was the early Elvis records, along with those of Roy Orbison, Carl Perkins, Johnny Cash, Jerry Lee Lewis, Billy Lee Riley, Warren Storm, and Ed Bruce, who came out of Sun Studios in Memphis, that got me really wanting to play music.

I formed my first band, the Empaladors (I don't know what it means either, it just sounded good), when I was about thirteen or fourteen years old with some friends of mine from high school. We played school assemblies, talent shows, school dances and proms in and around north Mississippi. On Sundays we'd drive thirty miles down to Houston, Mississippi, to WCPC radio station where Ralph and Robin Mathis, the owners, would have groups come and sing live from two o'clock until five. We would just sing the hits of the day. It was there at that radio station that we recorded our first song. It was called "Suddenly There's a Valley." It was just a cover song that had been a hit some years earlier by Gogi Grant. Anyway, they played our version on the radio there, and it started to draw requests. It got so many requests that it was number one on the request line for about four weeks. I used to hear it every morning before I went to school. Now I was really in high cotton. That was my first taste of any kind of musical success and I liked it. Number one for four weeks on WCPC, a fifty-thousand-watt station. We thought we'd hit it big even though there were no records to sell in stores or to send to other radio stations. We also played the local VFW club. We made eight dollars apiece for four hours' work on Saturday nights. That was two dollars an hour. It sure beat the dollar an hour that I made working summers at the Pontotoc Power Association as a grunt. That appealed to me, too. I also wrote my first song around this time: "I'm a Fool."

And then—there were the green rolling hills of north Mississippi. The land, the dirt, the woods, the pastures, the beautiful oak trees and honeysuckle and muscadine vines. It got in my blood, under my skin and is still in my heart and soul. And there were the people: family, friends, neighbors. All good, good people. These things worked together in harmony to help shape my songs and my life. And there was Mom. She was always encouraging me, never ever discouraging me. That meant so much to me even though I didn't realize it until years later.

I loved growing up in Mississippi. I have been blessed.

Fred Banks

Fred Banks, former Mississippi Supreme Court Justice, was born in 1942 in Canton
where he attended parochial and public schools, graduating from Lanier High School
in Jackson. He received his undergraduate and law degrees from Howard University.
A former legislator and trial judge, he is now in private practice of law at the Phelps
Dunbar firm.

W ithout the education and inspiration my teachers gave
me during my childhood, in two very different educational settings, my career would have likely turned out
very differently. Perhaps, like my father, I would have run a funeral
home. Or, I could have worked for the post office, a relatively secure
and favored position in my community at the time. But I didn't. I attended Howard University in Washington, D.C., and became a lawyer
and then a judge and now, again, a lawyer. My parents and the opportunities created by the civil rights movement aside, the blessings of
my professional life began with those teachers.

I began my education in a Catholic missionary school for black
students in Canton, Mississippi, in about 1946. I say about because
I don't remember whether I was three or four in my first encounter
with Holy Child Jesus. My mother, a registered nurse, worked at that
time, sometimes twelve hours a day, doing private nursing duty. My
father ran a business as an embalmer, funeral director, and burial insurance agent. Neither was Catholic. I believe that they sent me to the
Catholic school because that school took children at a younger age,
and because they thought that a better education was to be gained

there than in the Canton and Madison County public schools which they had attended. Neither of my parents went to college. My mother did nursing training at Grady Memorial Hospital in Atlanta, and my father finished embalming school in Chicago. Nevertheless, they both had a keen appreciation for education and directed me toward college and beyond from the beginning. As my grandfather used to advise, "Get it in your head and they can't take that away."

The teachers at Holy Child Jesus, and later at Holy Ghost in Jackson, where I attended third through tenth grades, were primarily white nuns of the Holy Spirit Missionary Sisters (S. Sp. S.). They hailed from a number of states, north and south, and from Germany, some with strange-sounding names like Sr. Charitosa and Sr. Arseniana. From pre-primer, as it was then called, through tenth grade, I had only three black classroom teachers—a female fourth-grade teacher, a female algebra teacher doing her practice teaching, and a priest who taught religion starting in the eighth grade.

Holy Ghost High School, founded in 1918, was the first high school for blacks in the city of Jackson, predating Lanier, the first black public high school, by seven years. It was also the first to be accredited by the Southern Association for Secondary Schools in 1943.

Holy Ghost was something of a racial enclave in the segregated Mississippi of the 1950s. A white priest and a black priest lived together in the same rectory. Not much to speak of until you realize that as late as 1969 white city council candidates offered as an excuse for maintaining an all-white fire department the fact that firefighters had to spend the night together at the fire station. We had to sue the city in the '70s to get the first black firefighters.

A couple of black lay elementary teachers taught alongside the white nuns in the '50s and, of course, we all went to mass together every Sunday. One year, probably the year after *Brown v. Board of Education* or perhaps even before, some of us recall that a white girl attended the elementary school for a short while, without reported incident, years before the first school desegregation in the public schools of Mississippi.

That is not to say that Catholic education was free of racism. Our ninth grade teacher, Sr. Thomas, a native of Georgia, was fond of admonishing us on those occasions when we became a bit noisy, as ninth graders tend to do, with the stern exclamation: "And *you* want to integrate!" I will always remember her for that and, in a more positive light, now, for the fact that she was the first person to notice my failing vision and insist that I get eyeglasses, which I have not been without since.

Putting the occasional missteps aside, I have no regrets over the Catholic education that those dedicated nuns provided me in my formative years. They taught me discipline, the basics of reading, writing, and arithmetic, and an attitude of tolerance and respect for all human beings. Looking back, however, I believe that I was also profoundly influenced by the black teachers, especially the male teachers, to whom I was exposed during the two years I attended Lanier High School in Jackson.

I started Lanier in the eleventh grade. While I lived only a half block from the school, I did not transfer there for convenience or just to pursue a broader educational experience. The fact is that, even in those days, Lanier was a basketball powerhouse and, unlike Holy Ghost, had an indoor gymnasium. It also had a full array of sports, while Holy Ghost fielded a team only in basketball. As a youngster living in the vicinity, I also had friends at the school who were sports stars whom I looked up to and admired.

Along with most of my friends at that age, the world of sports obsessed me. That's not unusual, regardless of race. But professional sports, recently desegregated, had become important to the spirit of the black community in that era. The first hardbound book that I remember receiving was one about baseball players, given to me by my grandfather in the late '40s when I had just begun to read. It was the age of Jackie Robinson, which began in the late 1940s and followed upon the heels of the celebrated exploits of Jesse Owens in the 1930s and Joe Louis in the 1930s and 1940s. By the mid-1950s, Bill Russell was leading Boston to championships in professional basketball, and

Jim Brown was doing the same in Cleveland in football. It seemed that athletes were leading the way to an open society for us all.

So, when the Lanier basketball coach let it be known that I might have a chance to play basketball at Lanier (he probably thought that I was a ninth grader who might grow, rather than a vertically challenged eleventh grader), off I went to be a Lanier Bulldog. I got my wish. I made the basketball team, which won a state championship (without my playing much at all but rooting hard from the bench), and I played on the baseball team as well. But I got more than that. I did get that broadened educational experience.

During that first year Mr. Melvin Wiggins, along with several other black men and women, taught me in academic courses and lessons in life. Mr. M. J. Lyells, Mr. H. M. Thompson, and Mr. Richard Harris taught me history, math, and science. Mr. Alexander and Mr. Edwards taught me physical education; Mr. L. T. Smith and Mr. Harrison Barnes coached me in basketball and Mr. Alexander in baseball. Mrs. Dorothy Young taught biology, and Mrs. Geneva Brown Blaylock and Mrs. Alberteen Mason taught me English. Mr. Will Anderson, my father's classmate at Lanier, taught me trigonometry and conducted the early morning advanced math class my senior year in which, too often, I found myself too sleepy to fully comprehend. It is to these teachers and role models that I attribute a broadening of my horizons and worldview.

M. J. Lyells was an elderly history teacher. His classes were never that exciting but he had a fondness for reciting "Invictus" by William Ernest Henley, impressing on me forever the admonition that "He who knows nothing of the past has little understanding of the present and no conception of the future."

H. M. Thompson taught me algebra II. A very accomplished fellow, he later taught mathematics at Jackson State University and became Grand Master of the M. J. Stringer Lodge, the largest black Mason group in our state. Mr. Thompson's class excited me and he always kept us on our toes. He began with the maxim that in mathematics "what almost is ain't."

Richard Harris taught chemistry and physics. He is cited by some as a prime example of formerly black schools like Lanier losing their best teachers to formerly white schools with the advent of desegregation. The basic complaint is not a view to which I fully subscribe; the fact that it was said speaks to the high esteem in which Mr. Harris was held.

But Mr. Harris made his greatest impression on me with his musings about life and the race issue rather than science. In addition to making disparaging remarks about his own race, more for effect than anything else, he had choice remarks to make about the public school system and life in general. He often remarked to us that "all you have to do is show up around here and you automatically get a C because that's the public school system." If you wanted a better grade you had to actually do some work. "Whoever said that anyone went 'crazy' from working too hard was a liar, making excuses for the lazy." In a very humorous fashion, impossible to capture by mere words, he emphasized the duty to keep an open mind about our condition, the way things are, and the way they ought to be. He warned us not to rely too much on what the popular media had to say about such things as "communism" or the "American way" without a critical examination of our own.

These teachers played a very significant role in my education and my worldview. Their very presence inspired me—not to teach but, nevertheless, to achieve. Times have changed. More opportunities are available to African Americans to make their mark. That fact and other conditions have taken a toll on the availability of black teachers, especially black men, in our schools. Still, there is no endeavor more important to our community than that of teacher.

Noel Polk

Noel Polk was born in Picayune in 1943 and lived there until he went to Mississippi College as a ministerial student. For better or for worse he saw, or lost, the light on the road to D'Lo on a trip back to campus and decided to pursue a career as an English professor. He has published numerous works on William Faulkner and Eudora Welty. He has taught English at the University of Southern Mississippi and now Mississippi State University. He's taught in France, Poland, and Japan, and lectured extensively in this country and Europe. He has two children, three grandchildren, and a fiancée.

I. J. (*Ignatius Josephus* we heard and believed and repeated, but nobody had the nerve to ask because believing it made it all but too perfect) Smith: an anomaly out of Henleyfield: balding, tall, thin, and holding himself with a kind of stiffness that wasn't self-consciousness so much as the learned demeanor of people from the country who go to college and then make their livings in town in a starched white shirt and tie. He held his face and the back of his head ramrod even with his chest and his spine; we joked that he couldn't see his feet without bending at the waist, but the truth was—the joke went on, in sniggering variations—that he probably had only minimal interest in anything below his waist. He was too stiff to be lanky, but the lanky was there, undeniable but under strict control and not to be tolerated, certainly not at school. His face was narrow from top to bottom, ruddy as though always freshly scrubbed, almost cherubic, and there lurked in his eyes always a gleam of out-and-out pleasantness—it too under strict control though often breaking out into a muted risibility, an actual joke he told or heard, that was somehow at

77

disconcerting odds with his stiffness and with the weight of the mission he carried into his classroom. He was not terrifying in his physical presence, but in our certainty that we would never satisfy his high standards. He censored with perfection. He beat us over the head with expectation.

He taught junior and senior English at Picayune High School and he may, finally, be the most important person I encountered there. He and Charlie Newman, the band director, the only other candidate, were polar opposites: I. J. was stately, dignified, decorous, internal, eternally serious; tall, deliberate, focused. Charlie was short, squat, loud, flamboyant, a jazz drummer, and a creature of the improvisatory moment. Both were eminently character types whose personalities fit their callings exactly, and they appealed to opposite sides of my soul, like the angel and the devil on Pinto's shoulders in *Animal House*. What Charlie cared about was that we have some fun, play most of the right notes at roughly the same time as everybody else, and keep mostly in step with the others; what I. J. cared about was that we take life seriously, be able to conjugate verbs in all tenses and moods, and above all, know the vital connection between life and the conjugation of verbs. Though Charlie was then and has remained the greater friend, my Baptist soul always pulled me toward I. J.'s more convincing deep seriousness about life and literature.

To him, literature was a serious business about serious matters, and to study it required only slightly less devotion and energy than one would give to the scriptures; until then I had thought reading was for fun, not for duty. In our junior year he required us to memorize old ponderous William Cullen Bryant's cheesy meditation on death, "Thanatopsis," to declaim all eighty-one morbidity-thrilled lines to the class, then to undergo his and our classmates' critiques of our performances: at stake was not just the accuracy of our memory but also our delivery of the rhythms, the enjambments and caesuras that enabled the poem's *deep meaning* to appear. He was visibly moved when one of us gave what he called a particularly expressive reading of the line, "old Ocean's gray and melancholy waste." Forty years later

I can still give an impressive account of "Thanatopsis" for as many lines as anybody will stand still for, though nobody recently has lasted for more than five or six lines, I'm happy to say.

The front of his classroom was a sort of stage, raised about a foot or so above the floor, which extended his natural height and made him seem even taller and more distant, and as he talked or read aloud, he deepened his voice just a bit and slowed his speech, as though in declamation, to be completely—*completely*—understood. He addressed us as "Mister" and "Miss," the only one of our teachers to do so, though what we heard was less respect than formal courtesy, a deliberate pedagogical decision to treat us as adults or at least as serious students and to expect an equal seriousness and accomplishment from us. His voice was sepulchral and weighty with accusation, even when that risibility broke through, as in: "*Mist*-er Polk. And just what is syntactical redundancy?"

Our senior year he presented us with a ghastly lineup which, to us, took up where "Thanatopsis" left off: *Moby Dick, Pilgrim's Progress, Robinson Crusoe,* and *The Scarlet Letter*—an odd and somber combination of morality and consequence for kids most of whose glands, bursting at the seams, gave slightly less than a fig for morality or consequence either. In his rigid allegorizing he—and I, of course—were firmly committed to the principle that the white whale, the natural creature, was as evil as Ahab said he was and therefore deserved the scourging the good captain and we set about to give him. Hester Prynne, of course, got no more than she deserved, while the guys, like Harold Hill, hoped and prayed for our local Hesters to win at least one more A. I never heard the names of Faulkner or Welty or O'Connor from him or anybody else in Picayune. Indeed, I never learned from anybody at Picayune High that anybody anywhere had written anything since 1850, *much less* that anybody in Mississippi had done so.

Almost all my classmates despised and repudiated him, they said, but they hadn't yet reached the levels of deep seriousness that I. J. and I had. It was not then surprising, and is even less so to me now, that most of my friends didn't enjoy his classes; it would astonish me to discover that any of them ever dipped into *Pilgrim's Progress* for an evening's entertainment or that they ever read much of anything else. I can't in fact claim that I actually *enjoyed* his classes (there were plenty of times when even I, as Tommy Stewart often put it, would have gone to hell twice rather than go to his class), and it took even me some years to rediscover that reading could be actually pleasurable rather than just instructive.

Language too was a serious business, a creature to be corralled and controlled lest it betray us into error. He didn't even allow Shakespeare much latitude: when we enacted *Macbeth* on his stage, he insisted that "out damned spot" be changed to "out cursed spot." Language that slipped at all slipped into the profane and inevitably carried us with it. Thus, interspersed between sorties to harpoon the white whale and to pull ourselves out of the Slough of Despond, I. J. taught us English grammar with all the devotion and intensity of the classic schoolmarmish teacher of Latin. He was the kind of English teacher everybody seems to have had, the one who gets so bound up in language's rules that they become some standard of morality or performance by which folks can and should by God be judged and mostly found wanting. He was, that is, the archetypal English teacher, the one who still causes adults, grown professional men and women, to shudder and grow sick at heart when they learn that I am an English teacher: "Oh?" they say, then shuffle their feet, look embarrassed, and for some reason feel obliged to confess: "I'll have to be careful around you. English was my worst subject." All English teachers have dealt with refugees from such as I. J., who see language as a prison of sorts and he, such as he, the unforgiving judge, jury, and jailor; or maybe just a trap, a snare, which we English teachers have laid for everybody. English teachers have thus become, willy-nilly, our culture's superego, the language cop everybody's happy to escape, who keeps us forever in a default relationship to our own language: forever in arrears, forever abandoned and ashamed, forever frustrated by our own tongue.

To I. J. the English language was beautiful in its structures, in its solidity, its balanced and symmetrical perfections, its securities in a 1950s atomic world that even we in boondocks Picayune knew was increasingly abstract and alien. Words for him had specific and powerful meanings that we could extract only by paying strict attention to their proper relations with language's rules. Oh, he would grant connotation and metaphor and occasionally even irony, but on the modernist and deconstructionist sense of language's slipperiness and deceptiveness he would have turned a severely disapproving eye. Or perhaps he was more modern that we knew, and it was precisely that slipperiness he feared, that kept him circling the wagons against the ragtag modernist onslaught of language's constantly deferred meanings, its leakages through the torn seams of communication. He taught as though words were containers already filled to the brim with all the denotation and connotation they could handle, and that we changed or misused them at our peril; as though the history of language had just stopped, ca. 1950, or so, complete and perfect.

To teach us our language he forced upon us rule after rule governing correctness: he never met a split infinitive or faulty parallelism that didn't signal the decline of Western Civilization. He was not concerned with the felicity and grace of a well-turned phrase but with *meaning,* the deeper, the more serious, the more profound, the better. He pounded the rules home to us daily in elaborate paragraphs we copied in special notebooks as he wrote them on the board or read aloud to us, and in grueling nightly hours-long assignments of verbs to be conjugated perfectly, not one jot or tittle out of place, in all tenses and moods, and sentences to be diagrammed. The next morning we worked through our homework in class on the blackboard, putting our diagrams on the board so that all could make visual and concrete the relationships between nouns and verbs, adverbs and adjectives, relative pronouns and antecedents, coordinate and subordinate connectives and clauses, between subjects and predicates, dependent and independent clauses, parallel elements of all kinds. Our final exam my junior year was one assignment, to diagram the Bible's Great Commission: "Go ye therefore, and teach all nations, baptizing them in the name of the Father, and of the Son, and of the Holy Ghost: Teaching them to observe all things whatsoever I have commanded you: and, lo, I am with you always, *even* unto the end of the world" (Matthew 18: 19–20). He didn't even write it out for us, but assumed, expected, that we all knew it by heart.

All of this was damnably tedious, all of it taxing, all of it basic, and nearly all of it, alas, utterly gone from English teaching today, except perhaps in some lonely outposts where folks my age and older still believe that language study requires the same discipline and even rote knowledge of formulae as, say, the study of chemistry does.

I ran I. J. to earth at his home one Saturday morning; perhaps I had an excuse, perhaps not. Henleyfield is about six or seven miles northwest of Picayune, and he lived out from Henleyfield, with his brother, also a bachelor. I found him sitting in a rocking chair on his front porch, barefooted and in overalls, staring out across the road in the direction of the stand of corn he had planted; he wore an almost subliminal, and almost idiot sweetness on his face, as though away from school, town, he transfigured. He seemed happy enough to see me, hospitable; we chatted for a moment on the porch, then he invited me inside the house to show me the centerpiece of his living room, an old fashioned pump organ. He sat down and with his bare feet pumped the organ into life and played hymns from the *Broadman Hymnal*, sang, smiling broadly, and invited me to sing with him. We harmonized on "Whispering Hope," "Out of the Ivory Palaces," "The Old Rugged Cross," and others. He was more animated, more relaxed, and more human, than I had ever seen him. When I left he walked me to my car and watched as I drove off. On Monday morning, it was as though Saturday had never happened. No bonding or kissing up allowed.

But because of that morning and because he had offered so much advice on our oral deliveries of "Thanatopsis," I asked him, when I was to fill the pulpit at the First Baptist Church on a Sunday evening when the pastor was to be out of town, if he would come hear me and critique my performance. More kissing up on my part, of course. He would, he said. He came in just as the service started and slipped into a pew near the front door, where he solemnly sat and listened, without moving; he slipped out just as the final amen sounded. The next morning he said, simply, "Perhaps you should have chosen a different topic."

He had never been one to give high grades. During my years, lots of people got B's and C's from him who normally got A's (though I got B's and C's who normally got C's). I don't know whether his standards got higher after I left Picayune or whether his students got worse or simply more courageous (or desperate). He became the object of massive student and parent resistance to his unyielding high standards—impossible standards, they said. Principal and Superintendent put pressure on him to ease up. He refused, no doubt with a very stiff neck, and finally resigned rather than yield to the pressure or listen to the complaints; he retired to Henleyfield, his corn, and his hymns. Twenty years after I graduated, I sent him a copy of a book on Faulkner I had written, with an inscription to the effect that at least one of his students was very grateful for what he had done. Of course I expected a response, a simple heartfelt note, an acknowledgment of some form of connection, English teacher to English teacher, across the years. I got none. No doubt he noted one too many syntactical redundancies or thought I needed another topic. Or, indeed, perhaps Faulkner didn't fit his definition of literature. Twenty years later, just recently, as a matter of fact, I published a version of this essay in a pamphlet distributed at a high school reunion in Picayune. One friend of those years said she had read what I had had to say about sending I. J. my book and wanted to tell me that she and I. J. had been friends (a fact I never knew), that he had brought my book and its inscription to show her, that he was proud, and that he wept, but confessed that he didn't know how to respond. And now to all the other enigmas about him, I add my inability to understand why a simple "Thank you" was somehow too much for him to bear, somehow more than he was capable of.

I've never been sure why he didn't beat "English" out of me too, as he did out of so many others. Upon his advice, I decided to major in English in college rather than in Religion or Bible. To be an English major fit my plans to head for the ministry; I was to postpone theological studies until I got to the seminary in order to get a broader background as an undergraduate. And since as a minister I was to be a public speaker, an English major would give me discipline and lots of practice in organizing and expressing my thoughts. In the short run, that English major helped undo my plans to enter the seminary by putting me in contact with minds less deeply moralistic and somber, though no less serious, than I. J.'s.

In the long run, his lessons have mostly stuck with me: not those about literature's seriousness, though God knows there's enough of that, not his insistence on rules but his sense that the rules have an important function and that a working relationship with those rules is essential to good writing, good reading, good teaching—and good living. Somehow I finally learned what he apparently never did, though he made it possible for me to learn it, that words and rules work toward meaning—toward poetry, I mean, not toward morality, not so everlastingly toward seriousness of purpose—when they are jazzy and improvisatory rather than rule-bound, an octopus rather than a crab, a playground rather than an a fortress. I. J. did not teach me to read but he did teach me to write. Charlie gave me music's discipline by teaching me its freedom. I. J. gave me language's flexibility by teaching me its rigor.

John Maxwell

John Maxwell, born in 1944, has performed his one-man play *Oh, Mr. Faulkner Do You Write?* for over twenty-five years. He is the founder of Fish Tale Group, a nonprofit organization dedicated to enlivening scripture through drama. He tours churches with his religious monologues based on characters from the Bible. Born in Pickens, he now lives with his wife Sandy in Jackson. His son Townes attends the University of Mississippi School of Law in Oxford.

I was born in Jackson in 1944 and lived all of my early years, until college, on a cotton farm two miles outside of Pickens, Mississippi, just past the RESUME SPEED sign. I have many early memories of growing up on that farm.

Well water was always cold, even on the hottest of days. Sugar cane was delicious, especially when Daddy cut it into cubes so it was easier to chew. I was absolutely certain that someone lived in the floor furnace, and that there were little people, somewhere, living in the radio, though I was never able to find them. The wisest people I ever knew in my boyhood were old black women.

It was not a good idea to fill up my daddy's pickup truck with water where others had filled it up with gasoline (I thought I was doing Daddy a favor). The best place to hide when you had misbehaved was under the house right behind where the chimney extended through the floor, and fried chicken always tasted better if you were eating the gizzard snitched from the stove before it ever got to the table. But perhaps the most indelible memories I have in my childhood were those of the Big Black River. The Big Black River held mysteries that could give you both joy and nightmares.

That river could yield a huge catch of catfish on a trotline that had been stretched across the water from one bank to another with hooks baited with goggle-eye. The trick, you see, was to tie one end of the line to a willow tree so that when a big channel cat or blue cat took the bait, it couldn't straighten that hook out by pulling on the line. You'd set that line out in late afternoon and check on it the next morning before school to see if there was a prize waiting for you. All you had to do was to look at the willow. Was it swaying back and forth? If it was, you knew *something* was on the line. What that was, was another thing altogether, and thereby lies the nightmare.

As a boy growing up in the South, you were never afraid of anything. This was the unspoken Code of Little Boyness. Of course you were afraid of a lot of things, but you never let on that you were. Even as you sat on the front row of the Mavon Theatre and watched *The Creature from the Black Lagoon* with both eyes shut, or your hands in front of your face, peering through your fingers every now and again until you couldn't stand it anymore, you still would never admit you were scared. On this particular night I was staying at my grandparents' house, and coming back from the theatre I had to walk by Worthy Funeral Home where there was a light on in the very back room.

"Somebody died today, and they're working on 'em," my wide-eyed friend Tony said. We shut our eyes and held our breaths, then ran as fast as we could until we got completely past that funeral home. Even then we did not admit we were scared. You'd have fistfights with your friends if anybody ever accused you of being "a'scared." It just wasn't to be, if ever you were to claim yourself a real boy and not a sissy, which was the ultimate insult, other than saying something derogatory about somebody's mama, which meant mandatory conflict. Girls were scared of everything, and completely useless in your eyes. And it would give you great delight to hear them scream with terror when you attempted to drop a bullfrog down their dresses. Girls were scared. Boys were not. This was the first law of the Little Boys' Ten Commandments.

Anyway, after standing there on the edge of the Big Black and watching the willow tree swaying, my heart would jump, as I knew something was on that hook. I just didn't know what. And it could be anything. ANYTHING! You see, my best friends Tommy and Tony had suggested that some of the fish that lived in the deepest part of the Big Black had teeth that could bite through steel and that toothless ones could swallow you whole. And since it was so deep in places of the Big Black, there was no light, so that some of the fish had no eyes, and were bigger than the biggest barn we had ever seen, and these fish would just open their mouths and swallow whatever was put in front of them.

So it was with this bit of psychological baggage that I followed Daddy down the bank of the river, climbed into the boat and ventured out onto the water. Daddy would row, and my job was to pick the line up and troll to the hook; then Daddy would put the paddle down, and come take whatever it was that we had caught off the hook. There was, most of the time, a low fog that hovered on the Big Black, and this didn't help with the trepidation that had built up in your quivering soul. As we slowly approached the hook, the one that had a beast of some kind on the end—a beast that had had the entire night to work up agitation and ire and would want to wreak vengeance on anything it suspected had played a part in its present dilemma and that probably had a particular appetite for little white boys—I sent a tiny prayer up to the Almighty. I had been taught to do this in Sunday school just as "Meshack, Bedrack, and Debendigo" had done before being thrown into the fiery furnace.

"Lord, please let whatever it is on the end of that hook either have just eaten, or be good-natured, 'cause I don't want to wind up in the belly of a catfish—spending the rest of my young life like Jonah." (Was Jonah fishing on the Big Black when he was swallowed by the whale?)

Let me say here, too, that all of my wisdom at that young age was acquired from observations and deductions from conversations with my twin buddies Tommy and Tony. The three of us knew all there was to know about life, or what we made up to be the truth—'specially about China. Yes, that's right, we all had theories about China. When we went on vacations together to the Gulf Coast, for instance, and stood there looking at the gulf, it was always China that you'd swim to if you could get to the other shore. Just as it was always China that you'd hit if you dug a hole in the ground so deep you'd come out on the other side. "Why don't you just go to China?" This could mean absolutely anywhere. But about the Big Black, we had all decided that parts of it had no "other side" at all—that there was no China there because some of it was so deep it was bottomless.

So this is all to say that no one could lay claim that I was not suitably prepared for what I was about to experience as Daddy and I continued to troll down the trotline, closer and closer to the HOOK. The closer we got to the HOOK the heavier the line. You could see the water beginning to roil and stir as if there were something huge churning just beneath the surface. And the line was getting heavier and heavier now—so heavy, in fact, that I realized I was not sitting anymore, but partly standing—squatting—with the full weight of the beast about to pull me into the water! Daddy must have sensed that I needed help and reached over and grabbed the line. The look on my daddy's face when he took ahold of that line and felt how heavy it was did not help the trepidation I was feeling in my heart. "Damn!" my daddy said. My daddy never cursed (at least not in front of me he didn't) and when he said "Damn!" I knew we must be in trouble. Deep and serious trouble. So Daddy grabbed the line and we both inched down to the infamous hook. When we finally got there my daddy looked at me with, "Now when I say, let's both lift!"

There used to be a Dr. Pepper in Pickens (that's right, his name was actually Dr. Pepper) who had palsy. When you went to Dr. Pepper to get a dreaded shot, as he held the syringe in his hand, right before sticking you with it, it would shake "like a bowl full of jelly." Hitting the right spot in your arm was always a crap shoot. Up to the moment when I was to help my daddy pull the beast on the end of that hook out of the Big Black, that had been the most painful moment of my young life. Not anymore. Dr. Pepper had found his equal.

Daddy looked at me. "Now lift!" We both heaved that hook out of the water (it took us both to lift it) and momentarily—just momentarily, as it was too heavy to hold for long—I got a glimpse of the beast. It was the scariest thing I had ever seen in my young life. Scarier than sitting in the waiting room waiting to see Dr. Pepper. Scarier than *The Creature from the Black Lagoon*! You see, this wasn't something I was looking at on a big screen—no, this was something I was staring at that was *real*! It was a ninety-pound gar. A gar looks like a long skinny shark. This one was about five feet in length, and most of it was teeth. And it came up out of the water looking straight at me! Like it blamed *me* for the fix it was in. And it was not happy. It was not happy at all. "Ahhhh!" I screamed. "Grab the line, son! Don't let go!" "I ain't grabbing nuthin'!" I said, and started trying to paddle for the shore. My daddy started struggling with the fish, trying to pull it into the boat. "Help me with it, John. It's not going to do anything. It's a gar! It's not going to hurt you. Help me get it in the boat." "But it's got teeth, Daddy. Real teeth! Sharp teeth! And them teeth can bite. And it's looking straight at *me*!" I yelled this out, as I continued to paddle and Daddy continued to hold the line, keeping the boat from going anywhere. "It's the biggest gar I've ever seen," Daddy said under his breath. "Doggone if this ain't the biggest. I declare! I declare!" Then to me with determination, "Come on, son. Don't be afraid."

Well, that did it there. I stopped dead still. Turned to my daddy. *Don't be afraid!* I couldn't believe my ears. This was serious, that my daddy would think I was afraid. This was painful. This touched the very soul of "The Little Boy Book of No No." "I ain't afraid! I'm just— just—!" "You scared to death!" my daddy shouted. "You 'bout to pee in your pants." "Naw, I ain't!" My daddy knew very well what he was doing. It was the only way to get me to help. And it worked. Was I a man or a mouse? Was I a sissy or a little boy? Was I going to turn my back on the Code? My daddy had said I was afraid. My *daddy*! Well, I turned to that fish, bit my lip and reached out and grabbed the line.

Me and my daddy pulled and pulled on that fish—finally my daddy had to wrap his arms around the middle of the gar and haul it into the boat. At last! At last the beast was grounded. We piled it into the boat, and I immediately scrambled to sit on the tail end of the fish, not wanting to get anywhere near those teeth and those eyes. We both collapsed down with a thud onto the seats of the boat. For the longest time we didn't do anything but just sit and pant—pant and stare at the gar, its gills pumping, too. It had been a fight. "Call *me* afraid," I muttered to myself. My daddy had a gleam in his eye.

The fish flapped a couple of times, making a loud noise thudding against the boat. It flopped big-time for a while trying to bounce itself over the side of the boat back into the Big Black—but the fight was over. The gar knew—we all did—that it was over. Finally, after a spell, I looked at Daddy with the question, "Will we eat it?" There wasn't much I had not eaten as a country boy growing up in Mississippi. I had eaten rabbit, squirrel, pig's feet, possum, brains and eggs, chitlins, pot likker, mud cat, and all sorts of fish and birds.

But that gar? "Somebody will eat it," Daddy said.

As we rowed back to the shore with our unbelievably large "catch of the year," I couldn't do anything but stare at it. It had seemed so fearless in the water, and now it seemed so helpless. And it's funny—I know this is going to sound strange about a gar, but as I stared at it, I almost came to respect it. It had a fearless look in the water, and it probably ruled the river for a while, putting down eel and snapping turtles and the like, but it had run up on a hook baited with goggle-eye, and a willow that would bend, and it had met its match. It was almost too much to eat it. It needed to be stuffed and put somewhere. "You don't stuff a gar," my daddy muttered. "You mount a big bass, or something you catch out of the ocean, but not ever a gar." Huh? Too bad. Something that big and that fierce that nature had given so much to—not to end up, at least, on somebody's wall somewhere—but that's the way it would be, I guess—just a glitch on nature's scale.

The gar was here for the briefest of times. Just like the summer we caught that fish and the years that passed so fast afterward.

Constance
Slaughter-Harvey

Constance Slaughter-Harvey was born in 1946 and is a native of Forest, where she graduated in 1963 from Hawkins High School as valedictorian. In 1967 she earned a bachelor's degree in political science and economics cum laude from Tougaloo College. In 1970 she became the first African American female to receive a law degree from the University of Mississippi. Her accomplishments include serving on the Governor's Minority Advisory Committee under William Waller; as Regional Presidential Team Coordinator for party nominee Jimmy Carter; as Fair Hearings Officer for Mississippi Health Planning and Development Agency under Cliff Finch; as a Presidential Scholars Commissioner appointed by President Jimmy Carter; as Executive Director of the Governor's Office of Human Development in the administration of William Winter; as Assistant Secretary of State for Elections and Public Lands; and as head of the Mississippi State Democratic Party Coordinating Campaign, coordinating campaigns for all Democratic state-wide candidates. Currently, she has a private law practice in Forest and is a columnist for the *Scott County Times.*

I turned eleven years old during the summer we spent in Westwood, California, where my father was attending the University of California at Los Angeles (UCLA) while working on his master's degree in administration and education. Mama, three of my five sisters, and I accompanied him to Los Angeles. Daddy was not allowed to attend the University of Mississippi, Mississippi State, or the University of Southern Mississippi for his master's because of his race, and Mississippi's education department paid for his tuition and expenses to attend an out-of-state university. Neither Jackson State nor Alcorn University had graduate programs at that time.

It was my responsibility to keep records of all expenses on the trip so that Daddy could receive reimbursements for reasonable expenditures. I learned at an early age to document well and to keep receipts. One would only have to look at my home, office, library, car, purse, and my IRS tax files to realize that I have a penchant for receipts.

The journey to the University of California via Route 66 was an introduction to the realities of life. We started our trip with excitement as youths venturing from the South to the West, and I was certain we would see the "wild west" or at least some reminders of my favorite cowboys and horses. We played the "zip game" where you score points by spotting horses. Not only did we not see the "wild west," but we saw instances of wild racial inequities and injustices.

For instance, Daddy drove from sunup to sundown and stopped at a hotel in Flagstaff, Arizona, which had a flashing neon sign indicating "vacancies." After reading and rereading the *Negro Travel Journal* as we rode, I knew that "vacancies" meant available rooms. Little did I understand what was about to happen. Daddy got out and went inside, only to return with a strange and disturbed look on his face. He told us they were full and we'd have to look further for a room that night. I'll never forget the look on his face when he got back into the driver's seat of our 1954 orange and white Dodge sedan.

I later learned that the white manager had said he had room, but not for us. Thanks to the *Negro Travel Journal*, we were able to find a place to sleep that night. Years later, Daddy and I would revisit the Flagstaff vacancies experience as I prepared motions in the Home Extension Services desegregation lawsuit.

Of course, there were good memories on Route 66 as we traveled to Westwood. We especially enjoyed the Petrified Forest, the Grand Canyon, the Painted Desert, and a meeting with an Indian mother and child along the roadside. She was reluctant to have her picture taken unless we purchased pottery. Mama understood this mother's need to protect her child, and she encouraged us to purchase a bowl even though none of us liked the dish. Despite having to sleep in the car one night, we managed to enjoy the rest of the Route 66 trip to Westwood.

When we arrived at the UCLA/Westwood campus, we encountered problems, but Daddy addressed them with little aggravation, and we moved into the family housing unit. We experienced forms of discrimination that caught Mama and Daddy a bit off guard. These were not unusually different from certain practices at home. We just didn't expect the problems in a venue in the West. I will not delineate all the specifics; suffice it to say that the problems of discrimination there were real and patent just as they were back home.

While there, we developed relationships that endured for many years. My older sister Cheryl and I were introduced to the business of babysitting, and she earned spending change for her efforts. I don't remember getting paid for having a good time with "little Andy," who was a year-old Hispanic boy. It was during that summer that I developed a love for the hot and spicy "real" Mexican food, especially hot tamales, and Andy was a joy to babysit.

Mrs. Sadie Welch was another person with whom I developed a loving relationship. I enjoyed being in her presence. She was my friend Elaine's grandmother who was visiting from Rochester, New York. She was sixty-five, had spotted white skin, and gray hair with a blue tint that no doubt came from a bottle. She would sit in her chair and tell me about her teenage years, and I would ask questions about our differences. I ran errands for her, and I especially enjoyed going to the store and getting fruit and snacks for us to enjoy. I stayed in touch with Mrs. Welch until her death in 1979. I had always looked forward to receiving her letters.

It was an enjoyable summer until we heard from our sisters at home that Daddy's parents had sold their homestead of more than forty acres on Pear Orchard Road in Hinds County for less than $150 an acre. When Daddy learned that a white woman named Mrs. Harper had spoken to his parents on several occasions behind closed doors, he became angry, just like he had been at the Flagstaff motel.

He was unable to convince them to return the money even after assuring them that he would borrow the money from the bank to save the land. I never knew my daddy to cry before, and if you had known this man of strength and determination, you would understand what crying in front of his children really meant. That loss of family legacy made a difference in his life. He developed stomach ulcers and was temporarily hospitalized for leg problems. Fortunately, we were able to return to Forest via Route 66 with Daddy doing most of the driving and Mama serving as navigator.

While the Route 66 trip to Westwood taught me much about life, in retrospect, it made me more aware of reality. I also learned much about human interaction while I played with Andy, listened to Mrs. Welch, and learned from Mama and Daddy and Cheryl (Cherry). I grew closer to my younger sisters, Clarice (Reccie) and Carolyn (Cal), and I missed playing with my middle sisters Charlotte (Luddie) and Cynthia (Cindy), who remained behind with our grandparents because the state of Mississippi would only reimburse Daddy for the expenses of four children. Discrimination with a fixed number—a stark reality. Several years later, Mama and Daddy would sacrifice and purchase forty acres in the city of Forest which they vowed would be left to their children and grandchildren. The experiences of that summer most definitely affected my parents and consequently affected my life and my daughter's life.

There have been many, many meaningful summers in my life, including the summer of 1964 when I worked at Head Start and grieved over the discovery of the bodies of Chaney, Goodman, and Schwerner, and the summer of 1965 when I participated in the Intensive Summer Studies Program where southern African American college students were introduced to the Ivy League life to see if we could survive. I did survive Harvard with two Bs and lifelong relationships with Mr. Walter T. Dixon, an African American city councilman from Baltimore who was my classmate in Introduction to Constitutional Law, and a white family, Roy and Diane Hamer, for whom I would babysit little Daniel and escape the Harvard yard mental plantation. Then there was the summer of 1966 when I served as camp counselor at Camp Trywoodie in Poughkeepsie, New York, and developed lasting relationships with several persons, including Barbara Hunt and Lavern Davis, the granddaughter of Ruby Dee and the late Ossie Davis.

The summers of my youth were always quite interesting and all obviously influenced my life. The summer of 1957 spent in California, however, stands out as one that directly affected my vision and my choices in life. I am thankful for the examples Mama and Daddy set as a testimony to their strength, endurance, and visionary optimism for the beneficiaries of their legacy. It is my hope that my daughter, Constance Olivia, continues to embrace these traits so that the "Flagstaff vacancies" experience will be worth the pain and indignities we suffered.

Jimmy Buffett

Jimmy Buffet was born in Pascagoula in 1946, grew up on the Mobile Bay, and went to college at the University of Southern Mississippi in Hattiesburg. Multitalented, he is known best as a songwriter and performer of his own works which reflect his love of the tropics and salt water. His long list of hit songs includes "Margaritaville," "Come Monday," and "Cheeseburger in Paradise." He is also a best-selling novelist, a memoirist, restaurateur, pilot, and movie producer.

The ocean has always been a salve to my soul. During my childhood on the northern shore of the Gulf of Mexico, much of my summer vacations, free of the grasp of the Mobile parochial school system, was spent at my grandmother's house in Pascagoula, Mississippi. My cousin Baxter was my best friend, and we did what most pre-teenage boys in the fifties did. If we weren't building forts, we were reenacting the Battle of New Orleans, with one side being the British and the other the combined forces of General Andrew Jackson and the pirate Jean Laffite. Our charges and countercharges up and down the muddy banks of the small bayou that bordered the rear property of my grandparents' house inevitably would produce a corps of walking wounded. My grandmother had patched up a lot of children and grandchildren, and we would limp to the back porch of her house for first aid. She would nonchalantly patch us up with Bactine and Band-Aids, then pour a bowl of hot Creole gumbo into us for stamina and send us off to the real source of healing—the sea. She told us that the gumbo and Bactine would help, but that the best thing for a cut or an abrasion was to go swimming in salt water.

We took our grandmother's advice to heart, and off we would pedal on our old Schwinn bikes to the swimming spot near the Coast Guard base. I remember well the apprehension I would feel easing my skinny, prepubescent body into the water, waiting for the sting as the salt made contact with the fresh wound. But it did work. The next day scabs would quickly form and the healing process would begin.

Later down the road of life, I made the discovery that salt water was also good for the mental abrasions one inevitably acquires on land.

George E. Riggs

George E. Riggs was born in Hattiesburg in 1946, grew up in Laurel, and graduated from Richton High School and the University of Southern Mississippi. He began his newspaper career at the *Hattiesburg American*. Today he is president and CEO of California Newspaper Partnership (CNP), a corporation jointly owned by Media News, Gannett, and Stephens Media. CNP, the largest publisher of daily newspapers in California, publishes ninety-five newspapers with a total circulation of 1.5 million throughout California, including the *San Jose Mercury News, Oakland Tribune, Los Angles Daily News, Contra Costa Times*, and others. Riggs was honored on December 7, 2007, by the California Press Association as Newspaper Executive of the Year.

*S*ometimes, the most powerful influences in our lives aren't the friends and loved ones around us, but events into which we're thrust and the strangers with whom we share them.

It is early morning on an August day in south Mississippi, still cool and quiet, but the humidity is already gearing up for another stifling day. I am in the tiny town of New Augusta, waiting for the 7 a.m. Greyhound bus to Jackson, where I am to be drafted into the army. It is 1968, and the war in Vietnam is raging. I am alone as I wait, I assume the only passenger on this day. So I sit on a bench, thinking of the events that brought me here and wondering what lies ahead. The bus arrives and I put out a cigarette and board. There are only three or four other people on the bus, spread randomly throughout the cabin. I take a seat a couple of rows from the front, well away from the others, and sink back, still lost in thought.

Two weeks earlier, I had been in Buras, Louisiana, working offshore as a roughneck. Located on a thin sliver of hurricane-swept marshland fifty miles south of New Orleans, Buras is sort of a latter-day Hole in the Wall. A tough, hardscrabble oil field town, it attracts the kind of men who do work that is dangerous, hard, and dirty in return for good wages and few questions. Years later, in 1981, Norman Mailer helped an aspiring writer named Jack Henry Abbott get out of prison. Within six weeks Abbott had stabbed a waiter named Richard Adnan to death in a New York alley and went on the lam. Buras was where they finally caught him.

I had made lots of trips to Buras. When I had money for gas I drove. When I didn't, I hitched. By the time I was twenty-two years old, I had been working in the Louisiana oil fields for several summers, as well as during spring and winter breaks between semesters. I was a student at the University of Southern Mississippi in Hattiesburg, working my way through school. A few times, when financial necessity compelled it, I had dropped out of school entirely for part of a semester, withdrawing from classes with an incomplete and heading for Buras.

Dropping out was a dicey move, however, as it meant possibly losing one's coveted 2-S student deferment from the draft, and instead being given 1-A status—eligible for immediate induction.

In earlier years, while the lottery was in effect and when I first started working offshore, dropping out meant playing draft roulette, your fate dependent on those strange balls that were drawn to determine who with which birthdates would be inducted. So, you could drop out of school and go work offshore, lose your student deferment, and still most likely not get drafted. It was a game lots of guys played. One, a professional card player from Mobile, registered every semester, never attended classes, then withdrew with an incomplete for all classes before midterm exams. The next semester he would do it all over again. He never got drafted.

In my case, it was simply a matter of needing money for tuition and living expenses, having run out before the semester ended. I began my first summer in Buras as a roustabout, or unskilled laborer. I did every type of labor imaginable, from slogging through swamps laying pipe to helping dig and plaster a swimming pool. Some jobs lasted a day or two, some several weeks. The routine for finding work in Buras was pretty simple. You showed up at Sheffield's Café early in the morning, ordered a cup of coffee, and waited. Eventually someone would come in and announce in a loud voice, "I need two or three men to lay pipe" (or any number of other manual jobs, cutting weeds, chipping and painting, digging trenches, etc.). If you wanted the job, you got up, paid for your coffee, went outside, and climbed inside the waiting crew truck. No background screens. No drug testing. No questions. You were hired on the spot.

After several weeks during my first summer, I signed on for something called a "mud run." I had no idea what it was, and really didn't care. I was young and strong, and figured whatever it was I could handle. It turned out that a mud run was some of the most backbreaking work I had ever done. It meant going offshore to one of the many drilling rigs in the gulf to unload barges loaded with sacks of dry drilling chemicals. Back then, drilling rigs used a mixture of several types of dry chemicals that were mixed with water and pumped into the hole while drilling. These came in fifty- and one-hundred-pound bags that looked like sacks of cement, and were delivered to the rigs on large barges, several thousand bags at a time. The bags had to be manually offloaded from the barges and placed in a "mud room" inside the rig, where they were mixed.

So a half dozen other laborers and I huffed and puffed throughout the day and into the night, hauling sacks from the barge up a gangplank-style walkway and onto the drilling rig, down the metal stairs and into the mud room, where they were stacked. When we finally stopped for a lunch break after about five hours, one of the other roustabouts, a rail-thin, red-faced guy named Ed, opened his brown paper lunch bag and pulled out the only item he had brought for lunch, a pint of vodka. He opened the top, chugged about a third of the bottle, quietly put the cap back on, and lit a cigarette. Nobody said a word, including the crew leader sitting a few feet away silently chewing his sandwich.

This was our first time on an actual drilling rig, and after lunch a few of us went up on the rig floor to watch the work. I was immediately captivated by what we saw. When the rig was drilling, things were quiet enough. The workers, called roughnecks, went quickly about their duties, cleaning equipment and doing various chores. But when time came to pull the drill pipe out of the hole to change out the drill bit at the bottom, "going into and out of the hole" as it was called, seeing the work of the crew on the floor was jaw dropping. Pipe was pulled up in ninety-foot stands at a time, quickly disconnected, and placed vertically in a huge rack to one side of the derrick.

It sounds simple enough. But watching as the huge yellow block screamed skyward, hoisted by roaring diesel engines that lifted the pipe out of the hole and up toward the derrick man, who was leaning out from a tiny platform ninety feet above, and seeing the floor crew work the two pairs of giant tongs used to break apart the stands of pipe at floor level, the deck slick with the mud-like drilling chemicals, I found it all amazing. For me and a couple of the other laborers, who were also seeing it for the first time, the fear factor was off the charts. We looked at each other, eyes wide as saucers. I knew immediately I had to become a roughneck.

Two summers and half a dozen trips to Buras later, I had been roughnecking long enough to land a job on a big offshore rig fifty miles out in the gulf. We were drilling in three thousand feet of water, the rig positioned on top of a large platform, and the crews were living ten days at a time on board a ship tied off alongside the rig.

Ironically, one night as we were going into the hole, a contract mud crew, much like the one I started out on, came out to our rig to unload a barge of drilling chemicals. And during a break several of them came up to the floor to watch, just as I had done. We were working shorthanded as one of the crew took a lunch break, so I was operating both sets of tongs, a tricky situation that required holding one set locked in place with your foot while swinging the others into position and locking them with your hands. I looked up to see eight or nine very fresh faces, several of them obviously college guys, staring in disbelief as they watched us work. I laughed as I thought back to my first mud run, seeing roughnecks at work.

I had always been drawn to dangerous work, figuring, I suppose, that it was the quickest way to make money. After high school, I had worked the summer following graduation as a deckhand on a riverboat, moving wheat barges up and down the Mississippi. Later, I worked as a strikebreaker, crossing picket lines at a Masonite plant in Laurel, Mississippi. It was a tough strike in which at least one strike breaker, a former classmate of mine, was killed.

The main benefit of roughneck work, aside from the fact that it paid extremely well, was that living offshore enabled me to save virtually all my pay. Meals and sleeping quarters were provided, and thus if you were saving money for tuition and college expenses, as I was, it was pretty ideal.

However, one big downside was that ten days out in the gulf could often turn into a much longer stint, such as when the relief crew arrived shorthanded. Usually that meant the newest member of the crew, often me, had to stay over for an additional ten days to fill the opening. Then, of course, your regular crew arrived again ten days later, and you had to stay another ten days to get back on cycle. Thus, thirty days straight without seeing land, working twelve-hour shifts, then dropping into a bunk exhausted each night.

This lent an air of desperation to getting back on land. Being flush with paychecks and having the temptations of New Orleans only an hour away could also often lead to waking up days later in some strange places, without all of one's senses—or finances—totally intact.

It was a strange sort of existence, the kind that takes over your soul so gradually you never know it: working at a job that despite its menial nature pays very well, and doing it for months at a time with tough, hard-drinking men who spend their leisure time carousing in a city known for nonstop partying, then returning to the straight-laced regimentation of university life.

It was probably inevitable that I would start to find the student life increasingly boring. I gradually lost interest in every phase of school. I hadn't found a major I really liked, so classes were a walk-through. I didn't date much, as the rituals associated with it seemed absurd to me: meeting someone, asking her out on a date, picking her up at the women's dorm, where you actually had to sign her out for the evening—it was too much hassle. I could meet a girl in a matter of minutes any night in the French Quarter, and without all the complications.

There was also the fact that much of college social life at that time revolved around fraternities and sororities. A friend had once asked me if I would like to pledge his fraternity. I asked what was involved. He explained about the great parties and fun they had. But then he said, "You know, of course, that the members often give pledges 'licks' with a paddle at pledge meetings. How would you feel about that?" I responded, "If anybody tried to hit me with a paddle I'd throw him through a window." He laughed and said, "You wouldn't make a very good pledge."

He was right. I hung out with a cast of characters who lived on the edges of university life. Many were older and not students, or if they were, they weren't really engaged in campus life. So without realizing it, I had slipped into the life of a pseudostudent, drinking too much and running with a rough crowd while at school, then heading offshore to replenish my depleted savings, and increasingly looking forward to that more than returning to school afterward. I think in my heart I realized that I was wasting my life, but it was a cycle in which I had become increasingly comfortable.

The Vietnam War was the bane of every student's existence. It was omnipresent in the late sixties. If you were male, you worried about the draft and being forced to go to a war that few on campus supported or believed in. And even if you did not have to worry about being drafted—those with medical disabilities, for instance—you still had friends, or friends of friends, or perhaps family who were there, had been there, or were about to go.

For someone like me, who loved a good fight, or for that matter just about anything dangerous, Vietnam would seem to have been made to order. Instead of hanging around the periphery of college life, why not just join, give the army its two years and return to college afterward on the GI Bill? It crossed my mind many times. I knew a few guys who had done that, and it seemed at first like a great way to get an education. But there were several drawbacks. First, while those I knew who had taken that route had managed to return unscathed by the experience, all of us knew others who had not. Some came home wounded, some returned deeply troubled and, of course, the most unfortunate did not return at all. Also, not one of those I knew who had been to Vietnam recommended the experience. In fact, it was just the opposite. Their advice was, whatever it takes, stay in school, get out, get a good job and hope you don't have to go at all. As one close friend and former roommate told me, "Even if you get lucky, get a good assignment, wind up in Germany or some place good instead of Nam, it's still two years of your life completely wasted."

It seemed like good counsel. A few months later it was summer and I was working offshore again. I returned one night after a stint in the gulf to my usual address in Buras, the Popich Hotel. The next day I went to the post office to pick up mail, and there it was, my induction notice. I had been drafted. I was to report to the induction center in Jackson within a few weeks, just days after my twenty-second birthday. I remember feeling slightly numb, not afraid really—more a mixture of uncertainty mixed with relief. The waiting would finally be over because a path had been chosen for me. But what that path held, where it would lead and how I would deal with it were things I could not know.

So these were my thoughts as the bus rolled toward Jackson. We arrived several hours later as the midday August heat baked downtown Jackson. As I got off the bus at the induction center located on State Street, I realized that I was within a few blocks of my mother's tiny apartment. Mother had lived there for several years, working as a switchboard operator at the nearby Sun-n-Sand Motel. I loved her, but wasn't a very good son when it came to staying in touch, dropping by infrequently and calling or writing only periodically. I felt a twinge as I entered the induction center, suddenly realizing that even though it was only a few blocks to her apartment, and another block to her work, I might not be allowed a last visit with her before going to Ft. Pope, Louisiana. Ft. Pope was where all inductees went for basic training before being sent overseas. I entered the induction center feeling a mixture of queasiness and guilt that I had not made the effort to arrive a day or two early to visit her.

Once inside, I saw lots of guys my age and younger milling around and waiting, none talking much and all looking very nervous. It did not help my queasiness to look at their faces, ranging from mild fear and anxiety to stony-eyed blankness, each lost in his own thoughts. Many had acne, some looked weak and frail, others looked stronger, but none had that air of self-assurance one sees everywhere on college campuses. The majority appeared to be just kids from poorer, working-class Mississippi families. It struck me that, while others had the financial means to go to college, or the family ties and contacts to get into the reserves, these kids were what the draft net had caught—those without a means of escape.

Within a few minutes, an army sergeant walked into the room and asked everyone to stand. He quickly explained the routine, telling us what to expect as we went through the afternoon's physical exam. Once exams had been finished, he said, we were all to return and reassemble in the same room for further instructions. Then we were led to another room with lockers, where we undressed down to skivvies, placing our clothes inside the lockers. After that, the process was a blur of tedious paperwork, waiting in line, and shuffling from one area to the next.

Near the end we came to the hearing exam; it was in a booth with a glass door and was large enough for two or three people. I filed in with two others and sat as an army staffer explained the process, which simply involved pushing a handheld button each time we heard a sound and releasing it when the sound disappeared. After the test, the staffer opened the door, gave the others their paperwork, and told them to proceed to the next station. He then told me I had failed the high-frequency portion of the hearing exam, and would have to be retested.

This time I was left alone in the booth, and the test lasted much longer. Afterward, he opened the door and told me I had again failed, and that I should follow him to a doctor's office. We walked down the hallway to the doctor's office, and he handed my test results to an older guy who had very close-cropped hair on the sides and was balding on top and who was obviously an army doctor. He looked very fit and tough as whipcord.

After reviewing the results silently for several minutes, he told me that I would have to return in about a month to be retested at a separate nonmilitary facility. I asked if it could be done sooner, explaining that my mother lived nearby and that I could stay over. He said no, it could not, and that I would receive further information by mail in a couple of weeks. He told me I should go out and rejoin the group in the large room where we had initially gathered.

When I arrived back at the starting point, everyone was already there and standing side by side, still in their skivvies as we had been all afternoon, their toes along a white line that formed a giant square around the room. In the middle of the square stood the sergeant who had given us our initial instructions. I moved in and took a spot in line. He told everyone to pull their skivvies down to their ankles so that the staffers could give us hernia exams, and while they were doing so, he would give us our final instructions.

It was at this point that I noticed that several guys were crying, a few weeping quietly, as others sobbed openly. The staffers moved from one person to the next, inserting a finger into each groin and barking, "Turn your head and cough." Then they moved on to the next in line. The sergeant spoke slowly and deliberately, his voice strong and authoritative: "When we leave this room, you will return to your lockers and get dressed. After which you will line up at the door and follow me out to board the buses at the rear of the building. The buses will take you to Ft. Pope, Louisiana, where you will be formally inducted into the United States Army. After six weeks of basic training, you will receive your orders for duty. As you know, our country is at war, and most of you will be going to Vietnam. You will have a chance to visit your families again before you leave."

The tears flowed more freely around the room as the reality of what was about to happen sank in. My head pounded and I had dry mouth, even though I knew I would not be boarding the buses. I showed one of the staffers my papers, and asked what I should do next. He told me to get dressed and meet him back there. I dressed as if I were in a fog, not quite fully comprehending what had just happened. Out of the entire group, I was the only one that had failed the physical exam. When I returned to meet the staffer, the others were already lining up at the rear door to board the buses. The staffer led me through the line and down the hallway to the front door. He opened it and I walked out, alone, into the late afternoon Mississippi sunshine.

I started walking toward my mother's apartment, still dazed and trying to grasp my good fortune. Some of those I had just spent the afternoon with would die. Others would be wounded, some physically, others emotionally, by what they were about to go through. But by some inexplicable twist of fate I had been spared. I didn't know why, but I made up my mind as I walked down State Street that afternoon that I would not squander the opportunity I had just been given.

In the years to come, there were many people—teachers, friends, bosses—who helped me along the way. They were people who believed in me and gave me a nudge in the right direction, some sound advice, or the examples of good role models. They all helped me in ways large and small, and far too numerous to count. But none had greater impact on me, or helped me to achieve whatever measure of success I have enjoyed, than the strangers I shared that August afternoon with in the summer of 1968.

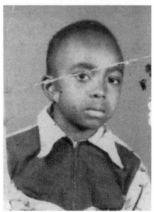

Clifton L. Taulbert

Clifton L. Taulbert, born in 1945, writes about the world that made him laugh, cry, hope, and despair—his world of the South. The central theme throughout his writing is "community." He writes to call us to that better way of being and becoming. His books grace the tables of supreme court judges and cousins back home in the Delta. He has been nominated for the Pulitzer Prize and was awarded the Mississippi Literary Award for Nonfiction. The bookends of the more than a dozen books he has written are *Once Upon a Time When We Were Colored* and *Eight Habits of the Heart*. Taulbert lives in Tulsa, Oklahoma.

"The rainwater was so high, we thought the road had become the river. As the waters continued to rise, so did my fear. We were scared. Houses floated off their foundations, animals were floating in front of our eyes and we heard of people who lived on their rooftops for days, praying to God for someone to come and rescue them.

"And in the midst of rain greater than any I had ever seen, the word finally got to us that the levee had broken in two places. The water from the river that had been held back for years rushed faster than the words of warning.

"My daddy said that in the city the soldiers were everywhere, keeping order and fearing for their lives. Mommy kept saying under her breath that the promise God made to Noah was being broken and she prayed for a rainbow that didn't come.

"In such a short period of time, our people were homeless and destitute and the rich and poor became a single race as their separate worlds merged into a single one of human fear. And that's the way it was," my great-aunt Elna said as she once again told me the story of the 1927 flood.

It was a story I had heard all my life as a young boy growing up in the Mississippi Delta, mesmerized by the lore.

For my aunt Elna, the flood of '27 was part of her life, a story of survival not to be forgotten, a story to always tell. And she and so many others did. For me, it was just history, part of the many front porch conversations that were part of our southern lives.

It was the story of old people, the story of their survival told to us, the younger generation, when we found ourselves concerned about the many obstacles in our paths. For many of them, their survival became their testimony of why we should never give up. Their stories of "we survived" passed from generation to generation and soon became the late-night stories told when sitting with the sick and dying.

Through their stories over the years of my life, I was kept in touch with the human suffering that characterized the 1927 flood and the aftermath. However, decades later, after growing up and becoming a writer and a storyteller like many of them, I would have the story of the 1927 flood again show up on my front porch.

This time, I would learn from fellow southern writer John Barry about the political and economic implications upon the states affected and the nation as a whole. It seemed as if the flood of 1927 would be the one natural disaster that would have no equal in our lifetime.

While sitting in one of the hundreds of magnificent southern pre–Civil War mansions in historic Natchez, I had a luncheon conversation with John in which I learned more about this natural disaster, the prospects for the city of New Orleans, and about the steel grip of separatism.

The 1927 era was a different time socially and this was reflected in the stories of rescue and recovery. Though there were a few stories of great humanity, the old people with whom I had grown up experienced few of them. It was indeed a difficult time for many of them. Though the forces of nature had revealed our common vulnerability as members of the human family, the prevailing social mores of the times were still quite evident, even in the midst of the destructive floodwaters.

Now, seventy-eight years later and into a new century, the forces of nature have again spoken loudly for all to see and hear, and from that mighty sound comes the echo of new stories for the front porches of this century.

Now I have my own tale, as the saga of '27 merges into the reality of 2005. I have become the storyteller, as so many others will, of great fear and great loss, when again the forces of nature moved faster than the warnings.

Hurricane Katrina and the New Orleans flood of 2005 has become the story for all of us.

I, too, will tell my great-nephews, great-nieces, and grandchildren of a time when the water was so high only rooftops could be seen, and animals floated, while people stood on their rooftops waiting to be rescued.

But unlike my great-aunt and her kin, I'll also have stories, hundreds of them, of unparalleled unselfishness as nature once again revealed our common humanity and our human vulnerability. I will share with them my witness to the intentional unselfishness of many of the American people who sought to build community wherever it was needed without regard to race, ethnicity, or the social standing of those in need.

Alberto J. Mora

Alberto J. Mora, born in 1952, and his family left Cuba during the revolution in 1959 and settled in Jackson, where Alberto attended St. Richard and St. Joseph Catholic Schools. He is a graduate of Swarthmore College in Pennsylvania and the University of Miami School of Law. In May 2006, the John F. Kennedy Library Foundation honored Alberto's service as U.S. Navy general counsel by awarding him the John F. Kennedy Profile in Courage Award, in recognition of his opposition to governmental policies and practices permitting detainee abuse. He currently serves as vice president and general counsel for the International Department of Wal-Mart Stores, Inc., and is a member of the Council on Foreign Relations.

"**A**ren't you John Devender's boy?" The question was put to me by a stranger as I was browsing through the racks at a clothing store in Jackson, a store I had first started frequenting when I entered high school in 1966, almost forty years from the date of the encounter. The gentleman was perhaps in his seventies: trim beard, starched white shirt, khaki pants, polished shoes, and straight back. A man accustomed to respect and no doubt deserving it. "No, sir, my father was Dr. Lidio Mora," I replied. The "sir" was not automatic, the way it had been when I was growing up in Mississippi, but it was required, and I attempted to modulate my voice so as to suggest that if he had not heard of my father, he should have. The man nodded and turned, apologizing for his mistake.

"Aren't you so-and-so's boy?" is a Mississippi question. It reflects a state rooted in tradition and habits, which in turn are rooted in its families and their traditions and habits. Growing up here, I knew my friends' fathers and mothers and grandparents, and had often heard about the great-grandparents and even earlier generations, too. A person wasn't just what he had done; he was also who his family was and family members were, what they had done, and the expectations one's parents and ancestors had helped create. Indiscernibly, these histories would become the guardrails of our lives, the signposts by which we would shape our characters. One of my classmates, a Harkins, would in middle age move an entire red brick Catholic church, which had been threatened by demolition, from its site in Leake County to his farm outside of Jackson. The church was not a notable structure, but generations of Harkinses had worshiped and been baptized and married in it, and that was a sufficient fact. Filial piety, family love, and respect for tradition mandated that the building be saved. That it was rescued in such an extravagant manner gave the romantic and quixotic gesture a very pronounced Mississippi stamp.

My family—consisting of my father, my mother, Klara, and my brother, Michael—was not from Mississippi or from the United States, for that matter. Father was Cuban and Mother, Hungarian. We came to the state in 1962 from Miami, where we had spent a year after moving from Cuba, exiles from the Castro revolution. In the city of Jackson, in that era, we must have been regarded as exotics. When my Hungarian grandparents were living with us, one could hear spoken at home, on any given day, Spanish, German, Hungarian, English, and at times, French. No less unusual, at least in our neighborhood in that era and in a state where the sale of alcohol was still legally prohibited, was that my parents kept a full bar and often served wine and beer at meals. My playmates were agog, at both our foreignness and the booze.

Father and Mother were the center of my life. Father was a physician, a gastroenterologist, who divided his professional time between teaching at the University of Mississippi Medical Center, the VA Medical Center, and his private practice. Lidio Mora had grown up one of twelve children in the green lushness of a tobacco farm in Pinar del Río, the westernmost province of Cuba. A passionate man who controlled his passions through discipline and moderation, he had two loves, one of which was medicine. He loved medicine so much that he couldn't read his medical journals late at night because he would not be able to fall asleep from the excitement. Always driven to excel, he had graduated at the top of his class at the University of Havana Medical School and shortly afterwards joined a Cuban medical team that was attached to the U.S. Army and provided medical care to civilians in postwar Munich, where in 1945 he would become the director of the city's largest hospital. Later, in postgraduate medical studies at Harvard, Father so impressed the editor of the *New England Journal of Medicine* that this doctor sought to enlist Mother, behind Father's back, in a futile effort to keep him at Harvard rather than allow his return to Cuba. He was strong, measured, compassionate, private, worldly, diligent, formal, sensuous, slyly humorous, and a good dancer. He must have suffered greatly at his separation from Cuba but, being a stoic, kept it inside. I only saw him cry twice.

Father's other love was Mother. Born into an old, accomplished family in Székesfehérvár, Hungary, Klara Pattantyus was raised in and molded by a world of manners, privilege, beauty, music, and culture that was swept away in the clash between the Wehrmacht and Red Army and the later imposition of Soviet tyranny over Eastern Europe. She is still beautiful even in her eighties, and Mother's fluency in five languages evidences a remarkable intelligence and disciplined mind. Aristocratic, spirited, strong-willed, elegant, confident, graceful, adventuresome, at home in the mountains, and an excellent cook, gardener, and decorator, she embodies the dash and strength of her father, Janos, a prominent lawyer in his community who had dueled with a cavalry saber, hunted boar, and combined a love of gypsy music with uncompromising standards and integrity. (It was Janos who taught me to eat caviar and raw bacon dusted with paprika and salt.) Uprooted from her family and country and frustrated in her ambition to become a surgeon by the upheavals of her generation, Mother was anchored by a limitless and helpless love for her husband and complete devotion to her sons.

After a year living in the old veterans administration complex, Father and Mother moved us to a home on Cavalier Drive. Michael and I were enrolled at St. Richard Catholic School, and we would complete our local education at St. Joseph Catholic School, institutions given their character by the largely Irish, and always demanding, Sisters of Mercy.

For the two Mora brothers, the process of becoming Mississippians was imperceptible. I have no memory of what the first step was, but it pleases me to think that it was in learning to say "Yes, sir" and "Yes, ma'am." Whatever else may be considered a necessary characteristic of a Mississippian, he says "Yes, sir" and "Yes, ma'am." By learning this habit, my brother and I became consciously respectful, learned of the hierarchy of age, station, and achievement, gained humility, and began to be integrated into a society in which publicly acknowledged respect for others is a defining and distinctive trait.

Our first neighbors—the Buford, Decker, and Sullivan families, among others, but above all, the Parkeses—provided friendship, food, affection, values, history lessons, and dogs to pet. Soon, other families that we would meet through school would add their imprints in varying degrees—McMullan, Cashion, Flood, Harkins, Joseph, Kestenbaum, Grower, Hutch, Fitzhugh, Luckett, Lange, McAndrews, and McCarthy, to name a few. Many of these families had old and deep ties to the South, some of them going back to the Civil War era and before. There was a broad range of personalities and accomplishment here: saints and the not-so-saintly; intimates of presidents and generations of governors and those without any political access or interest; the devout and those to whom religion did not matter; the well-to-do and those perhaps aspiring to the middle of the middle class; some who loved Mississippi and others to whom the relation was more tenuous; and hell-raisers and teetotalers. Years later, all these names still convey powerful memories and remind me of the truth that there is no such thing as an ordinary person. And as the Spanish poet Luis Rosales observed, those whom we love leave footprints in our heart.

Important, too, were the images and rhythms of life in Mississippi. Today—thirty-seven years after I moved from the state—I recall without effort the still green woods and shimmering heat of summer; running out for a pass on a front-yard football game; the rosin scent of a pine forest; the dry crack of a shotgun echoing across a stubble field on a winter day; the shocking violence of a bass striking a lure on a quiet pond; the first real kiss in the backseat of a moving car; the play of mockingbirds and blue jays; blackbirds sitting on an electrical wire and the black silhouette of crows slowly gliding across a tree line; the splash of scarlet at an Ole Miss tailgate party; the sadness of the Vicksburg battlefield on a rainy day; the smell of Pearl River mud; the roar of excitement as Archie Manning took the field against Alabama, or Tennessee, or LSU; the taste of a cold beer after mowing a lawn, when you were itchy with dirt and grass and covered with sweat; a brown cottonmouth on a muddy riverbank; the slippery floor of the basketball gym at a Friday night St. Joe sock-hop; the chatter of classmates in a darkened bus coming home after an away basketball or football game; and my friend Pat McMullan's delighted laughter— then as now such an important part of my life—as a gale capsized our sailboat on the Ross Barnett Reservoir on the afternoon of our senior prom, and our life preservers, carelessly left unworn at the bottom of the cockpit, were carried away by the wind.

These and a thousand other experiences while growing up defined me, even if I couldn't say exactly how. But I do know that when I stand on the reddish asphalt at the corner of Cavalier Drive and Old Canton Road and look around, I am overwhelmed by the involuntary realization that this very spot represents my emotional ground zero.

No, sir, my father was Dr. Lidio Mora—and I'm from here.

Edward Cohen

Edward Cohen was born in 1948, and grew up in Jackson, where as Head Writer for Mississippi Educational Television he wrote the PBS documentaries *The Islander, Hanukkah,* and *Passover*. His memoir, *The Peddler's Grandson: Growing Up Jewish in Mississippi,* was a Book Sense selection and won the Nonfiction Award from the Mississippi Library Association and the Mississippi Institute of Arts and Letters. His work has appeared in the *Oxford American,* and his play, *The Golem,* opened at Millsaps College. He lives in Los Angeles.

B eth Israel was not a reverent congregation. At the weekly Friday night services (all that remained of the traditional sundown-Friday-to-sundown-Saturday observance), the congregants' greetings, which started before the service, developed into over-the-pew gossiping once it began. At any one time during the service, eight or nine whispered conversations might be ongoing, with negligible peer pressure to be quiet. It was as if, unmoored from and unsupervised by the centers of Judaism in the North, all the adults became children eager to commune with their extended kin after a week of immersion in the Christian world.

Stepping inside the temple was like being transported to another dimension, one that was not defined by height or width or depth but by an equally pervasive factor, Jewishness. The transition was immediate. One moment I was outside, subject to all the perceived diminishments of the Christian world. The next moment, it all fell away and I felt like I was back at home on Brook Drive, in a much-expanded but equally all-Jewish universe. Once again, I knew that no one around me would make an anti-Semitic comment. The hermetically sealed worlds of Brook Drive, the canasta games, the temple, and vacations to Miami Beach and the Catskills were carefully constructed temporary fortresses where we might never have to meet a Christian.

As a child, I found it enormously comforting to sit with my parents, surrounded by Etta and Moise and the rest of the Cohens, in a room that held nothing but Jews as far as the eye could see. It was possible to pretend that the world was this way; knowing that it wasn't made the solidarity even greater. It was reassuring to see the canasta ladies, accompanied by their poker-playing husbands. After the service, everyone turned to those all around and murmured "Good Shabbas" ("Good Sabbath") and shook hands or kissed. As we made our way up the aisle to say "Good Shabbas" to the rabbi, some of the canasta ladies would enfold me with warm hugs.

Paradoxically, attendance at temple was often sparse. My parents went perhaps one Friday a month, sometimes less. The congregation was too small to exert the social pressure that nudged our Christian neighbors to their houses of worship on Sundays and on Wednesday prayer nights. Our temple simply didn't possess the gravitational pull to draw my parents out of their private Jewish island on Brook Drive. For us, Sundays at Granny's constituted religious service enough.

Though it seemed interminable to such a restive congregation, the Friday night service actually was fairly brief, perhaps an hour, depending on the rabbi and how seriously he took his duties to sermonize. It began with the kiddush, the lighting of the Sabbath candles, done by congregants summoned to the pulpit to struggle through the phoneticized Hebrew blessing with their southern accents, sometimes having to be helped over a syllable or two by the rabbi. There was a good bit of standing up and sitting down and long sections of narrative. For the responsive reading, the congregation was entrusted only with the English, while the Hebrew Union College–trained rabbi navigated through the Hebrew. I kept one finger in the back of the prayer book, watching the pages decrease at the rate it takes a watched pot to boil.

In shedding all the old-fashioned and embarrassing Hebraic mystery, the service had also lost some of its emotional heart. Yet some majesty remained in our pared-down, anglicized, and sparsely attended Friday night services. Despite myself, I would often be captured by the solemn poetry of the prayers, particularly the ones that seemed to speak of a special relationship with God and offered an explanation of why we had to be different.

The austerity of the temple's architecture was mirrored in the almost existential courage of the prayers. A religion that frankly states it does not know whether there is an afterlife brought forth my grudging admiration at the same time I resented the lack of any comfort. It was all intertwined with my mother somehow. When I asked her before she died whether she believed there was a heaven, she voiced the view I'd heard every Friday night in my youth: "You live on in the hearts of those who remember you." And that was it. What a responsibility for those who remained, and what breathtaking strength it required of the one about to depart.

At every Friday night service, the rabbi read the names of those whose *yahrzeit*, anniversary of death, had fallen that week. This commemoration was for me the most poignant moment of the service. When I was young, I recognized none of the names. Then, as I grew up, more and more frequently I did, and for the moment their names were read I would indeed remember them, see them—Lolita's round-faced mother, Rose, the frail sharp-eyed Mr. Martin, who had reminded me of Tottie, Victor Glick, who had no family and gave me his stamp collection—and so under Jewish tradition they would, at least for that brief time, live on. When the time came for Tottie's *yahrzeit* and for Rae's, my mother would always go to services, as did my father when Moise's and Etta's names were read. Because my family was normally so unobservant, their unfailing attendance emphasized for me what a sacred duty it was, this act of remembrance, the gift of life.

Midway through the service would come a private meditation. The prayer book gave an example but then stated, "or such other prayer as the heart may prompt." Sitting between my parents on the unadorned wooden pew, I looked to them for guidance as to what I should do in this uncharted section of the service.

My father's eyes as often as not weren't closed. When I thumbed to the back of the prayer book to see how much farther, he had already pioneered that journey and had his fourth finger firmly implanted there as a goal. If his eyes were closed, I could guess what he might be praying for—good business at the store, safety for my mother and me. But I could never fathom what my mother, closed within herself as always, might be praying for, some private thing that I would never know.

It is the memory of my mother that I most associate with Friday night services. When I was a child, my favorite place to be during the service was beside her when she sang in the choir. We'd walk up a narrow dusty staircase; musty, ancient-seeming, as if it had been there since biblical times, it was made of the same dark unadorned wood as the rest of the temple. I imagined such woods had constituted the interiors of the First and Second Temples in Jerusalem.

The choir sat in a small alcove above the pulpit. There my mother and two other volunteers from the congregation were led by a professional, a redoubtable-looking woman named Magnolia Coulet. No matter how many times I heard Magnolia sing, it was always a shock to behold her dexterous familiarity with the Hebrew songs, a fluency that far surpassed what most of the Jews sitting below could manage. She was a sweet-natured woman, and I felt somehow honored that she would have taken the time to master the intricacies of our secret language. Our club was so small that it needed as many members as it could recruit. My mother's singing voice was a clear, unwavering soprano, much sweeter than her speaking voice, or so it seemed to me. It was as if when she was safe in that little choir room, carried along with ancient songs familiar from her own childhood, she didn't need the edge in her voice that was her only protection against a hurtful world.

I, too, felt protected in that cozy alcove. I could peek over the top of the wall and look down at the top of the rabbi's bald head, then out into the congregation at my father. No one could see me. It was a secret kingdom, and with it came the sanctioned waiver of any requirement to follow the service. Whenever the choir sang, I sat, entranced by the metamorphosis in my mother's voice. Between songs, when the rabbi droned on below, I would listen to the choir's whispered conversations or drop off to sleep. It was deliciously illicit, like skipping school with no chance of penalty.

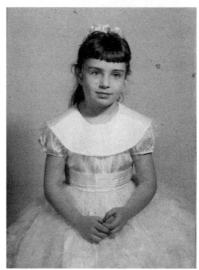

Carolyn Haines

Carolyn Haines was born in Lucedale in 1953 and grew up there in the newspaper business with her parents, Roy and Hilda Haines. She has published over fifty novels in
genres from literary to thrillers as well as short fiction and nonfiction. Two of her books
have been named in the top five mysteries for their respective years. She was awarded
an Alabama Council on the Arts writing fellowship and currently teaches creative writing at the University of South Alabama. She is active in animal rescue and has a family
of twenty-one "critters"—horses, cats, and dogs.

S ome people will be able to pinpoint one defining moment in
life when the path turned or cleared or dropped out from under them and set them on their present course. My story is different, because it is an accumulation of people and events that turned
me to writing fiction.

I enjoyed one of the last great childhoods of the South. Gothic,
dramatic, filled with crazy relatives, Christmas scenes from hell, family dinners of philosophical conversation, backyard baseball games,
bicycles, dogs, growing up in a haunted house, and parents and a
grandmother (who still retained her Swedish accent at times) who
were superb and devilish storytellers. No southerner worth her salt
lacks for gothic in her background.

Mayberry had nothing on the small town of Lucedale in the '50s
and '60s. My brothers and I could sneak out of the house at night and
ride our bicycles, carefree, down the darkened streets with our trusty
dog, Venus. To the dismay of our neighbors, we played hide-and-seek
in their shrubbery, the nearby woods, and a couple of abandoned

houses, where hiding was intolerable and dread mounted until at last we were "found."

We lived on the corner of Winter and Ratliff streets in a house reputed to be haunted. My mother gleefully told us stories of how prior owners had been driven out of the house by angry ghosts. She wasn't above filling a Playtex glove with damp sand, freezing it, and slipping it beneath a pillow at a slumber party.

My dad's specialty was a bit kinder. He made up stories of Leo the Friendly Lion and told them to us at bedtime, engaging the moments of courage and honesty and integrity.

My parents were journalists, and the written word was highly revered. Dinner conversation often centered around the importance of truth, the balance of fairness and intelligent exploration of an issue. While my parents encouraged the reading of all books, they were nonfiction junkies. Yet they encouraged the most prized of all writerly gifts—imagination. I played games and spun my own fantasies, which they listened to, embellished and encouraged.

My father taught me the importance of structure in any story. There had to be a skeleton, a spine, to hang the characters and events upon. A story had to move forward, whether it was a picture story (and I did love black-and-white photography!) or a story of words. I had no idea how important this would be for me later.

My expectation was that I'd become a journalist, which I did. After graduating from the University of Southern Mississippi, I worked for ten years at various southern newspapers. I met scoundrels, visionaries, nutcases, psychopaths, those whose souls had been corrupted by greed, and many, many decent people.

But it is the golden years of childhood to which I retreat for inspiration and a connection to place that is visceral. I can still taste the red dirt of a rural road. In the shade of Miss Hattie and Miss Mattie's old oak tree, the temperature dropped ten degrees on a hot summer day, and the gnarled roots contained wonderful hidey-holes. These moments, which engaged all of my senses, remain magical and important.

Because my mother worked at home as a correspondent, we children learned the value of staying outdoors. Her work was intense, a burst of typewriter keys flying, as she wrote up a wreck or drowning or board of supervisors' meeting. It was far better to be outside, playing in the nearby woods (as long as we didn't return bloody from some misadventure). In her insistence on quiet while she worked, she taught me another valuable lesson—that an atmosphere and time to write should be respected.

When she wasn't writing up news stories, my mother ran a sort of "clinic." People from all over the county came to her kitchen table to tell their stories and ask advice. Both of my parents were advocates for those without a voice. They believed that journalists were the watchdogs of the community. They acted on that belief, even when the cost was high.

The coffeepot was always on in the kitchen, and there was no telling who would show up at the back door with a tip for a news story, a tall tale, or a request for advice on a domestic or medical issue. My mom had a strange knack for diagnosing illnesses. She was an intuitive, with only the training of her personal experience. But those who needed help came to our door, and I would make coffee and serve banana pudding or chocolate pie or whatever Grandma or Mama had cooked that day.

By working quietly and efficiently in the background of the kitchen, I was allowed to stay in the room, and I heard many things that I shouldn't have. For example, my novel *Penumbra* grew from a tiny seed. I don't remember the woman, or even what she looked like, but she showed up in the kitchen confessing her affair with a traveling route man. She told my mother that she met him on the banks of the river and that she wanted to leave her husband but was afraid of the consequences. My mother cautioned her strongly, urging her to break off the affair or end the marriage. I never knew what happened to this woman, but this was the genesis of *Penumbra*, which begins with Marlena, unhappily married to the wealthiest man in fictional Drexel, meeting her lover at the river. As my mother predicted forty years ago, the consequences—at least in my fictional world—were dire.

While the memories have faded to vague impressions, I still re-member the woman's voice threaded with a compelling blend of joy and fear. She'd taken her life to the edge, and that's exactly where I like my characters. Even before I became a journalist, I learned the role of observer. Writers are snoops and eavesdroppers, and I had plenty of opportunities to practice those skills in a safe place. The emotional currents in our kitchen were powerful, passionate, and sometimes dangerous. Yet my mother was also there, a rock against the buffeting surf of trouble.

When I was in high school, I began photographing accidents, fires, drownings, the moments of human drama and tragedy. My father was an editor and worked in Pascagoula, and my mother had suffered po-lio as a child. Walking was difficult for her, so I became her legs. Get-ting the story was how we made our living, so when I volunteered to use the camera, I was taught to do so.

I think several things came from those experiences. One speaks to structure again, and the importance of skeleton—the composing and framing of the picture that tells the story. Another lesson that has stood me in good stead for all of my life is that of discipline. We worked every day. News didn't regard holidays or weekends as times of repose. It happened and we covered it. The deadlines were rigid, ironclad masters that were served even if Christmas dinner was held back for several hours. We wrote every day.

During my years of journalism, I found that I preferred writing feature stories over hard news. With features, I could play with lan-guage, creating moods and scenes—a luxury in the fast-paced world of news. I read voraciously, and I lived intensely the world of fiction into which I stepped.

Lucedale didn't have a bookstore, but there was a bookrack in a lo-cal pharmacy. Each month, after the rack was refilled, I started at the top and read my way to the bottom. I had no one to tell me what was "good" or "unworthy" fiction, so I read everything. I had the gift of being able to enter the world of sweet romance or haunted castles, or the more disturbing towns and adventures created by such writers as Thomas Williams, John Irving, and Robert Stone.

Reading in my high school classes was one of my notorious habits, and I'd managed to get one of my mother's best friends and the woman I was named for, Carolyn Nyman, as my English teacher for three years in a row. Carolyn was on to my habit of sticking a paperback novel in my English text and zoning out. I'd mastered gerunds, participles, and those tricky verbs back in sixth grade. I was home free in English—or so I thought until one day when Carolyn plucked my novel from in front of my English text and looked at it. She wasn't a woman who belittled her students. Instead, she asked me to stay after class.

I was expecting a lecture and possibly the threat that she was going to tell my mother. While Mama tolerated a lot of bad behavior, she didn't allow us to show disrespect for teachers, particularly not those who were her friends. Instead, Carolyn handed me another book. It was a collection of Eudora Welty stories. She said, "If you have to read, read something worthwhile."

When I got home that afternoon, I walked down to the woods where I liked to climb a tree and read. I opened the book to a story called "The Wide Net." I began to read about a place and people who were familiar to me. The river in her story could have been the Leaf, the Chickasawhay, or the Pascagoula. The characters were rural and spoke in the rhythms that fell on my ear like old friends. At that moment, I realized I wanted to write fiction, to tell the stories of the characters that peopled my world. I stepped from being a reader of fiction to a wannabe writer, one who would try to bring to life the complex relationships and shadings of character that have held my interest ever since.

That step from reader to writer is a giant one. During the '70s and early '80s when I worked for the papers, I wrote short fiction on the side, just for myself. I wrote because I couldn't stop. I was addicted to the vice. At a cocktail party on the Gulf Coast, I met Jere Hoar, an

Ole Miss journalism professor, who encouraged me to seek an agent. I signed with McIntosh and Otis, a literary agency, and began the long process of moving from short fiction to the daunting task of writing a novel. Today, I write the same way I read, in multiple genres, but it is the old South that holds my heart and my fancy.

Lorian Hemingway

Lorian Hemingway, the director of the Lorian Hemingway Short Story Competition, was born in 1951 and is the author of a novel, *Walk into the River*, a nonfiction book, *A World Turned Over*, and a memoir *Walk on Water*. In addition she has written for *Rolling Stone*, the *New York Times*, and other publications. The granddaughter of Ernest Hemingway, she grew up in Mississippi and now lives in Seattle.

One of the first fish I ever caught as a kid was a baby bass netted from a deep Mississippi ravine I lived in in summer. This was my refuge, that ravine, a place of discovery, revealer of miracles, its depth filled with a heavy current of reddish brown water during the spring floods, its red clay bottom dried to a pockmarking of deep holes by mid-July. I was tirelessly curious when I was young, bound inextricably to all natural mysteries behind four walls, nervous and jumpy if made to sit too long indoors, recalcitrant once sprung.

I'd watched this particular fish for days, trapped in a pothole in the ravine, swimming in a quick panic from one side to the other, instinctively seeking a tributary from its footwide prison. I empathized, imagined myself locked in my room for days, dizzy and breathless from claustrophobia, frantic enough to pull up the flooring with my bare hands. I understood feeling trapped, my life then nothing more than a crash course in how to escape. Escape meant steering past my mother, who sat limp at the kitchen table, stupid from vodka, or creeping past the time bomb that was my stepfather as he lay snoring, passed out in his recliner. I'd turn the handle quickly on the front

door and sink into the thick Mississippi heat, feeling, once I'd made
it to the ravine, as if I had, by sleight of hand, through sheer caginess,
become someone else. My head, which always seemed to buzz with a
jumpy current whenever my mother raised a full glass to her lips, was
clear.

Along the red clay of the ravine lip my bare feet moved with ex-
traordinary balance; I slid deep into the ravine bed without a sound,
a small avalanche of pebbles falling in my wake. I stood then surrounded by wide canyon walls, a young girl ready to trap the very
source of summer. I thought often it was the Cherokee in me that let
me move like an animal, quiet, steady, aware. My great-grandfather
had been a chief. His name was Golden for the strain of burnt-gold
hair and green eyes that surfaced every few generations. My mother
had the honey-colored hair, the green eyes. And then there was the
dark strain. Mine.

After a few days the water in the pothole had diminished by half
and grew so thick with ravine mud that the fish hung motionless in
the ooze, its gills laboring for the oxygen it needed. On my knees I
stared into the hole, goldfish net in hand, thinking it was evil, what
I was about to do, snatch a living creature from its habitat and bring
it, luckless, into my own. I remember the delicate thin striping on its
flanks as I lifted it, unresisting, from the muck, and how soft and filmy
the skin felt as I stroked a finger along its length. I remember, too, how
my heart raced as I dropped the fish into the jar, watched him sink
quickly and then just as quickly take his first breath in a new world.
Within moments he was moving through the jar as maniacally as he
had the pothole days before. I had given resurrection in a pint of water, become God to a fish. Years later I would remember that moment
as one of grace.

Fish became my fascination and began to appear in dreams, their
shadows deep in dark water, cruising, fins breaking the surface from
time to time, a teasing swirl of movement as I stood onshore with net
or rod or hands poised to strike. In one dream I stood before a pool
of monster fish with bare hands greedy, my fingertips singing the way

a line does when it's pulled free from the spool. As I leaned forward, a shape would slide deliberately beneath my reach, and I would lunge into water that was dense and thick as oil, only to come up soaked and empty-handed.

I don't know now that the dreams had to do with catching fish, but rather with some unconscious, archetypal need. I have consulted Jung on this one for the obvious, loaded symbolism. I have even dreamt, in these later years, of Jung, standing atop the stone fortress of his tower at Bolligen, fly rod in hand, a wooden piscatorial carving dangling from his leader line. He smiles in the dream, proud of himself. He did say that water is the unconscious and that fish are a Christ symbol. I deduce, then, from these boldly fitting pieces, that I am at times fishing for Jesus, or in some way, in recent dreams, dry-flying for Christ. I like the simplicity of it, the directness. I like that it speaks to Christian and hedonist alike.

But during those Mississippi summers that spanned my eighth to thirteenth years I paid little attention to dreams, mesmerized then by a world filled with fish, turtles, frogs, and lizards, anything remotely amphibian. Frogs were a class of fascination all their own, and I would capture them simply to feel the cool, crepey skin of their underbellies and watch the slow blink of their eyes. I progressed quickly from netting bass to catfishing with a bobber and worm, frittering away entire days on the banks of muddy lakes and rivers, certain, always, that the fish lived dead center, in the middle of the lake, assuming the notion that the truly elusive spend their time where we can never hope to reach them. To cast where they hid was my ambition. Eventually I understood that fish went wherever they damned well pleased, unimpressed by my clumsy form hurling hooks into their midst, immune to my need to know them. I had patience, the sort I suspect God has with people like me. It meant nothing to be skunked for days on end. I lived in perpetual hope of seeing that wayward shimmy of the bobber, then the quick dip and tug that signaled I had made contact with aliens. At that time in my life, *this* was my social interaction. I talked to the fish hidden deep in the ponds and streams I visited, trying to imagine what they saw beneath those mirrored surfaces, and reasoned it was hunger and not stupidity that made them take bait so crudely hitched to an obvious weapon. Compassion surfaced. I pictured scores of starving fish grubbing for worms, only to be duped into death by my slipshod cunning. When I'd haul them to shore I'd cry at what I'd done, at the sight of the hook swallowed to the hilt, at the flat, accusing eyes of the fish, and then I'd club them with a Coke bottle, the heavy green kind with the bottling company's name on the bottom. No one ever said there was another way to do it. In Mississippi, there was the hook, the worm, and the bobber, a holy trinity on a hot day in August—low-maintenance fishing I call it now. My guilt was usually pushed aside by their quick death beneath the bottle, and eating what I had caught seemed to remove the shame considerably.

My favorite fishing hole—I look back on it now as Mississippi's version of Mecca—was a place that to this day I am certain only one other knew of, the landowner who'd barbwired it off and posted a huge hand-painted sign along the fence—WARNING: SNAKES—a beacon to me. Yell "snake" and I ran not from, but *to* the source of panic, scooping the creature into my bare hands, trying to remember idly if red bands against yellow meant poisonous, or the other way around.

Roaming deep in a pine woods in rural Hinds County one summer afternoon, I came upon the pond, the edges of it rising in volcanic fashion from the otherwise flat land. I was accustomed only to ponds that were slipped like sinkholes into the surrounding pastureland, and as I made my way up the slight incline of earth, hands grasping the barbwire delicately, I beheld, not a rock quarry as I had expected, but instead a perfectly black pool of water, its dimensions no greater than those of an average swimming pool. At first I could not believe the color of the fish who were pushing to the surface, dozens of them, nosing one into another, their bodies opalescent as pearls, and huge, their lengths dissolving into the shadow of the pond. I had never seen albino catfish, had never seen *any* white fish, and thought for a brief, illogical moment that they had been segregated from their darker mates simply because of their color. In Mississippi then, it fit.

To have called this pond a fishing hole is misleading. I never actually fished its waters, too mesmerized by the cloudlike shapes that moved without sound through the deep pond, believing, beyond all fishing reason, that to catch them would bring the worst sort of luck. So I watched, alone in the woods with these mutants, some days prodding their lazy bodies with a hickory stick, which they rubbed against curiously, and on others merely counting the number of laps they made around the pond in an afternoon, hypnotized by the rhythm they made tracing one circle upon another.

The fish were as truly alien as my starkest imaginings, and I became convinced they were telepathic, reading my thoughts with such ease I had no need to speak to them. I called these journeys "visiting the fish gods," my treks to that mysterious water that had no business existing in a dry woods, and took into my life the memory of them, as if they were a talisman, granting me privileges and luck in the fishing world others could only dream of.

Sela Ward

Sela Ward was born in 1956 and is a Meridian native. She attended the University of
Alabama at Tuscaloosa before going to New York City where she worked as a commercial model. She moved to Hollywood to work in TV and feature films. She has won
two Emmys, a Cable Ace Award, and a Golden Globe Award for her work. She founded
Hope Village for Children in Meridian to provide shelter for children in need. In 2002
she wrote a memoir called *Homesick*.

The geography of my childhood is mapped in the streets and
yards of a green little enclave called Lakemont. Carved out of
a beautiful old 1920s recreational area called Echo Park, Lakemont was a perfect natural habitat for the packs of wild young baby
boomers who would soon be prowling its crew-cut lawns. My parents
had settled there comfortably in 1954, moving first into a single-story
ranch house, and then into a new brick-face split-level next door. The
houses were tucked away at the end of a cul-de-sac with a few other
sparkling new flat-roofed modernist homes—which, to anybody who
was looking, might have revealed something about their inhabitants.
My father was one of a loose collection of engineers and architects
who'd entered the Meridian workforce at about the same time, and
in the postwar years a handful of them colonized this little corner of
Lakemont, just a stone's throw away from their offices on the main
road.

On the surface it may have seemed like a typical suburban subdivision, but there was something about the connection among these
families that gave the place a sense of real community. "We all knew

each other," Daddy remembers. "Had the same background, education, worked on the same jobs." They all seemed to have so much
fun together. I remember the weekly card games my parents and our
neighbors took turns hosting: our house would fill with friends and
laughter, the men arguing philosophically as the evening grew late.
Mama always knew just the right thing to say; I marveled at her natural social graces, and wondered how I would ever learn what she
knew.

There were no mountains in Lakemont, just hills. But there were
two small lakes—ponds, really—and in the spring and summer they
became weekend gathering places for the entire neighborhood. Like
most people, when I recall my childhood what I am usually remembering are the weekends—warm and breezy, they all seemed to be, and
spent in a blur of tireless activity and blissfully uninterrupted leisure.
So many afternoons I spent sitting on the bank of one of the lakes,
with a cane pole in my hand, waiting for a bream to take the worm
on the hook. The little red and white plastic cork would disappear
under the water, and I'd give the pole a little upward tug, and haul in
the fish, as big as Daddy's hand. You'd see everybody there, Aunt Sara
and Uncle Boots and neighbors and friends, with their coolers and
lawn chairs and picnic lunches, talking and fishing, fishing and talking. When they drained one of the lakes, everybody—and I mean everybody—came to catch and eat the fish. It was like a communal feast.
This was not in the country, mind you, but in the heart of a modern
subdivision. Most of the men and women who lived there were Depression kids like my parents, and they weren't about to let those fish
go to waste. Besides, there isn't a southerner alive who doesn't love
fried fish fillets.

Not far from the lakes were a few scattered remnants of Echo Park,
which for us children retained the mysterious aura of things long
gone. By the time of my childhood they were largely grown over with
brush, but you could still see the entrance to the concrete cave that
had once been home to a bear named Chubby. CHUBBY BEAR'S CAVE,
as the faded lettering still reads, was a neighborhood landmark; we'd

crawl in, casting flashlight beams into dark corners to make sure no snakes were lurking, and then we'd scare ourselves to death holding miniature séances by candlelight. There was a persimmon tree hanging over the entrance to the cave, and when the fruits were ripe, we'd collect them as they fell. There were blackberry briars along the roadside by the cave, and we'd stain our hands purple picking the ripe ones.

When we weren't gathered around the lake with Mama and Daddy, we kids loved playing in the woods behind our house. Jenna, Berry, Brock, and I would build forts, sweeping the ground bare so we'd have soft dirt floors. We'd cut trails through the woods, and Berry would hunt birds with his BB gun. When somebody told him you could catch a bird if you put salt on its tail, he came up with a scheme in which he'd take a fishing pole with a plastic worm dangling on the end, dip the worm in salt, and try to touch birds' tails with the worm. I don't think the Lakemont birds were ever in danger.

Our neighborhood had a tennis court, and a swimming pool, where you'd see all your friends every day in the summer. There was an annual Lakemont picnic, with a potluck lunch spread three tables long, and all of those simple, old-fashioned games—sack races, bobbing for apples. When we weren't in the park itself we'd play flag football and Wiffle ball in nearby fields with our pals, ride our bikes up and down the streets, spend the night at each other's houses, and do all the things neighborhood kids did in the days before the invention of the scheduled play date. The only rule was to be home for supper before dark.

On a summer night there was no better adventure than to stay over with my grandmother, Annie Raye, the only one of my grandparents to survive into my childhood. She didn't have much money, and until her last years (when she moved in with us), she lived in a small apartment in a housing project in town. She smoked cigarillos, and read magazines like *Movie Mirror* and *True Detective Stories* with boundless appetite. I was never allowed to have coffee at home, but Grandma was always glad to sneak me a cup; she and I would sit at her little kitchen table, share a pot of coffee, and start our day together. I'd watch her forever, embroidering doilies and pillowcases, or working away at the old-fashioned, pedal-driven Singer sewing machine in her apartment. (I'm having all the little things she embroidered cut up and reassembled as a keepsake quilt for her namesake, my daughter, Anabella Raye.) I miss the hum of the oscillating fan at the foot of her bed; at night it would fill that quiet apartment and lull me to sleep.

My grandmother was also a wonderful cook. She made the most delicious fudge, dense and thick and rich. I've never had any like it since she died. She wrote the recipe down, but Mama always said she must have left an ingredient out, because it's never turned out quite the way it should. She also made *the* best corn-bread dressing for the holidays. The other day my aunt Nancy and I were remembering her leaning up against the stove on that crutch of hers, her long cigarillo hanging out precariously over the stovetop. "If you're looking for a missing ingredient," Nancy says, laughing, "you better think about that cigarette ash."

I was by nature a bashful child, and I rarely felt more secure and at home in the world than when I'd go into my grandmother's backyard, climb up into the mimosa tree, with its fuzzy blossoms the color of pink lemonade, and talk to it. I don't remember what I said to the tree, and it doesn't matter anyway. The important thing is that I felt the tree listened and understood me, achingly timid as I was, too fearful to pour out my heart to a living soul.

But I wasn't melancholy all the time. Most days I was happy to go look for something exciting to do. And I didn't usually have to look too far, because my father was always bringing something home that was way too much for us to handle. Once he gave my seven-year-old brother, Berry, a go-cart that must have gone twenty-five miles an hour; Mama almost had a heart attack watching Berry whipping around the driveway, his little head just barely visible over the steering wheel. On Saturday mornings we'd pile into the car and Daddy would take us chasing trains from intersection to intersection, blowing the horn and waving to the conductor.

If that sounds a tad dangerous, consider the other harebrained way we passed the time: chasing the bug truck. In the summer, the city would send a truck equipped with an insecticide fogger around town, spraying for mosquitoes. As soon as we heard the "fog machine" coming we'd go chasing it down the street, playing in the sweet-smelling cloud of insecticide smoke it left in its wake. It was probably aerosolized DDT, and it's a wonder we haven't all dropped dead of lung cancer. But I'll admit it sure was fun at the time.

Nowadays the neighborhood has aged, and there aren't many kids around. The levee we played on isn't often busy anymore, but I like to think that somewhere Mississippi children are still doing some lazy cane-pole fishing on a Sunday afternoon, not wasting their day in the mall or in front of a computer screen.

W. Ralph Eubanks

W. Ralph Eubanks's memoir, *Ever Is a Long Time: A Journey into Mississippi's Dark Past*, was named as one of the best nonfiction books of 2003 by the *Washington Post*. Eubanks was born in 1957 and received his B.A. from the University of Mississippi and his M.A. from the University of Michigan. He received a fellowship from the Guggenheim Foundation in 2007. The Mount Olive native is at work on his next book, *The House at the End of the Road: A Story of Race, Reconciliation, and Identity*. He lives in Washington, D.C., with his wife, Colleen, and children, Patrick, Aidan, and Delaney.

From the age of four up until right before I went to first grade, I went to work with my father. His office, which I viewed with great pride, was nothing but a cinderblock building, 14 feet by 18 feet, with a tin roof and a few windows to let the breeze run through on hot summer days. There was no bathroom; a wooded area nearby served that function. Above the front door to the office was an official looking weathered metal sign that bore the words, "Agricultural Extension Service: Negro County Agent and Extension Home Economist."

As you walked through the dusty wooden door flanked by two windows, there was a concrete slab floor where desks and typewriters were packed as tightly as the limited space would allow. Three people, in addition to my father, worked in the office: Andrew Reeves, the Associate Negro County Agent for rural development; Mrs. Annie Barron, the Negro Extension Home Economist, the wife of Mr. Buford Barron, the principal of Lincoln School; and Miss Mable Newell, the Associate Extension Home Economist. My father's desk was on the immediate left as you walked in the room. Across from his desk, in the center of the room, was a small typing desk and a dilapidated Remington typewriter, which was my spot when I came to the office. As my father did paperwork, I sat at my typewriter and did what I pretended to be my work, which were just silly stories that I made up or things I copied from a random magazine or newspaper that happened to be lying around the office.

If I wasn't at the typewriter, I sometimes sat on Miss Newell's lap. She was a large woman with a lap to match. One day I asked Miss Newell to marry me, and she accepted my proposal immediately. "Of course I'll marry you, Ralllph," I remember she told me. As only a southerner can, Miss Newell stretched out my name as far as it would go.

When she asked why I wanted to marry her, I said that it was because I loved her so much. But more than anything I loved that soft, comfortable lap of hers and the broad toothy smile she gave when she stretched out my name. When Miss Newell did get married I was heartbroken and fearful of her tall, seemingly gruff husband, Lamar Thompson, who I later found was just as kind and gentle as she was. When Miss Newell left the Extension Service, I made do with the stories I made up on my typewriter.

Mrs. Annie Barron was the opposite of Miss Newell. Annie Barron was a slight, thin woman who seemed to exist exclusively on soda crackers and Coca-Cola. Her diet was at odds with her profession, for she was a nutritionist and home economist who advised women throughout the county on proper nutrition and food safety. The county agents encouraged subsistence farming, and the home economists showed people how to improve their diets through farming.

Mr. Andrew Reeves was one of my father's classmates from Tuskegee. He was a native of Mount Olive and our families were very close. Often both families had Sunday dinner at our house, particularly during his wife's recovery in a nearby tuberculosis sanatorium. Mr. Reeves was a constant presence in my life, since I saw him almost every day except for Saturdays. Mr. Reeves and my father had divided up the county, so they rotated farm visits between them, with Mr. Reeves working the northern part of the county near Mount Olive and my father working the southern part of the county near Collins.

The time we spent in my father's office was minimal, although it seemed that I sat at that typewriter forever. Mostly we were out on the road doing field work, going from farm to farm, with my father putting his agronomy skills to work advising on crop rotation and diversification, recommending fertilizers for improved crop yield, and generally encouraging better land use. He also organized the Negro branch of the county's 4-H Club, gave advice on what to do with a sick cow or mule, and sometimes even treated the animal if he felt that he knew what medicine it needed. Other times he helped farmers vaccinate their herds against diseases such as blackleg, a fatal muscle disease in young cattle. I remember once there was a heifer with severe pink eye; my father cut out the cow's eye and sewed it shut. The farmer was forever grateful, since my father had saved his prize heifer and he told everyone he knew what a wondrous act he thought my father had done.

I made it a point to learn who lived around every corner of the winding country roads we traveled. The unpaved roads were dusty in the heat of the summer; after a hard rain, they were often muddy and rutted like a washboard. So, I learned where we were traveling not just by the landmark of a farm, but also by the feel of the car on the road. If we went to an unfamiliar part of the county, a part whose sights, sounds, and feels were unfamiliar to me, I would ask my father, "Who lives there?" He'd respond, "That's the Alfred McNair place, and everyone around each of these corners on this road up to the fork is a McNair," or "That's the McLaurin place, and Mr. McLaurin has one of the biggest herds of Black Angus cows in Covington County." Sometimes he might tell me something about the crops the people grew or the type of cows they raised. I gathered all of this information together so that if I returned to that road or farm, its look and feel would be familiar and comforting. When I drive down those roads today, they feel just as familiar, even though they have changed, as have a few of the names on the mailboxes.

My father and I visited the farms of black and white families, even though his title was officially Negro County Agent. Like Mississippi's school system, its education program for farmers, the Cooperative Extension Service, operated on the principle of separate but equal. The work of a Negro County Agent included service only to black farmers and sponsorship of black 4-H Clubs. Since my behavior would be a direct reflection on my father and his position, a strict regimen rooted in the code of manners kept me in line and kept folks from saying "that Eubanks boy just ain't gettin' no home training." But most of all, my father thought there were things I could learn from being with him that I couldn't learn at home under the feminine influence of my mother and sisters.

What he really taught me was everything I needed to know later in life, particularly in high school and college, about navigating through an integrated world. At the time, I sometimes felt overwhelmed, for many of the lessons my father tried to teach went beyond what I could comprehend. Yet in spite of my inability to grasp my father's lessons then, they have all stayed with me somehow.

Before we left his office to visit a farm, he would coach me on how I should interact with people. "Speak up and speak clearly when you're spoken to," he often insisted, since he felt I was too soft-spoken and needed to be more forceful. He sometimes admonished me for not looking up when I was shaking hands or not giving a firm handshake. "A man judges you by your handshake," he would remind me when I was feeling shy. These social rules were as important as the more practical ones like staying out of the way of farm animals or not playing with strange dogs. And I interpreted and followed them as if they were designed for my personal safety, which in a sense they were.

The behavior he expected from me around white people was the same as it was around black people: perfect. There was no double standard. In fact, from my limited perspective I saw no discernable difference in the way you behaved around black people or white people. You showed the same face to the white man as you showed to the black man. No mask was to be worn in the presence of the white man. White people were not mysterious creatures to be feared or to be emulated; they were just people. As a result, I learned the importance of being yourself and not what people or society wanted you to be.

Perhaps because my father was only one generation removed from a poor farm family, it was especially important to behave as respectfully in a ramshackle house of a poor black farmer as in the home of a prosperous white landowner. Although he never said it outright, from what I observed as I sat quietly on the sidelines, I knew he believed strongly in upholding the dignity of people, regardless of status. More directly, he taught me that my status as his son, the child of black professionals, was never to be used to separate me from those who may appear to be less well off.

Whenever I could, for as long as I could stand it, I tried to act like an adult. It was hard, but I did it because he wanted me to, and I would do anything for his approval. As a result, I knew there were times when it was fine to act like a kid and other times when it was not. Rarely was I allowed to be the center of attention, nor did I expect it. On most farm calls, my father instructed me to sit quietly and just watch what he did. So, in what seemed like a cloak of invisibility, at least one that made my noisy, fidgety little kid side invisible, I paid close attention to his every move. Later, back in the car, I asked questions. We talked about the crops on the farm or what he thought caused a cow's illness, but most of the time we talked about the people and whether he liked them or not. "It's not my job to like people," he told me once, "but it is my job to help them."

When he had to go to a remote corner of some farm, the family would often take me into their home as their guest. I had to be on my best behavior then—the best, that is, from a four- or five-year-old boy. I remember eating sweet crumbly molasses tea cakes in the simple yet tidy kitchens of poor black families, homes that bore pictures on the wall of Franklin Roosevelt and Jesus Christ, and, after 1963,

John F. Kennedy. I also sipped cold lemonade in the down-home elegance of the dining room of a white farmer, usually with the farmer's wife and occasionally with their children. In either setting, my hosts were to be treated with the utmost respect; no value judgments on my part were to be made about the social setting. Once during the ride home I made the mistake of mentioning that I noticed a hole in a wooden floor that I had to walk around to keep from falling in. "Don't ever judge people by what their house looks like," I remember my father said sharply. I don't remember very much else about that conversation that day, but I do remember the message: My father believed that any man who ridicules the poor is the one who is truly impoverished.

My father helped any farmer who sought his assistance. No one was given special status or priority and every farmer in Covington County knew it. In retrospect, he did much more than was expected in his job: Warren Eubanks could have earned his salary quite easily by working only within his defined territory, which did not include hands-on veterinary work or farming advice after hours. But doing things halfheartedly was not his way. Sometimes he even went out at night to help a farmer pull a calf, dragging me along to keep him company on the drive home to make sure he did not fall asleep.

When I went to school, the farm calls with my father ended abruptly. Although it was thrilling to go to first grade, school altered the rhythm of my life. Time with my father then centered around work on our farm rather than crossing the county together on our daily adventure. Though we still spent time together driving Mississippi from what seemed like top to bottom, like on our annual trip to the Delta to visit his old friends, those trips didn't feel completely carefree. As I grew older, other cares and concerns loomed as a backdrop to trips with my father. Little did I know that what felt like the jarring end of something in the mind of a preschooler only marked the beginning of bigger changes in my life and in Mississippi.

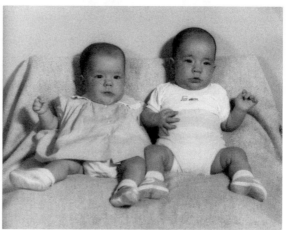

Sid Salter

Sid Salter, born in 1959, is a native of Philadelphia, Mississippi, and a graduate of Mississippi State University. He is a veteran political columnist and *Clarion-Ledger* Perspective Editor. In 2004, he was named MSU's National Alumnus of the Year. A former Ole Miss associate professor of journalism, he was the university's inaugural Kelly Gene Cook Chair in Journalism. He and his wife Leilani have four grown children and a young grandson.

Memphis—She never strays from a windswept hill overlooking the affluent part of this river city that gave birth to some of the South's hottest rock and coolest blues. I visit her there from time to time and remember her beautiful smile.

I shared every significant moment of my childhood—literally from birth to leaving home for college—with the best friend I ever had and the one person in my life whose love came to me unconditionally no matter how unlovable I became during certain periods of my life.

Sheila Salter Klimetz, my twin sister, was born seven minutes before me on a snowy night at the old Neshoba County Hospital in Philadelphia on January 16, 1959, near the present-day site of the Citizens Bank. My first memories on this earth are the sounds of her even breathing beside me in our baby bed and the weight of her body touching mine as she tossed in her sleep.

We were born two months premature. My mother was hospitalized for back problems and had been telling her doctor for weeks that she was pregnant with twins, but the doctor dismissed her protestations and told her he had only heard one heartbeat.

But Mama felt two heartbeats, two lives growing inside her. She knew.

When I was born, my mother said she looked at Dr. R. L. Moore and said: "I told you so." Dr. Moore apologized, but told her: "The girl is strong and ready to go home, but the boy is still struggling for his breath. We're going to have to keep him in an incubator for a period of time and help him along."

My father wasn't there. Thinking the birth was two months away, Dad was twenty-five miles from the hospital, in bed, fast asleep at our Newton County home. When told by his brother, who'd braved the icy roads to inform him, Dad chastised him for playing a bad practical joke.

Finally, a Philadelphia policeman confirmed to my father that he was indeed, at the age of forty-five, the father of twins—and he promptly ran outside with one shoe on and one shoe off into the snow getting to the car to make the trip to be with his family.

The familiar photograph that runs alongside my newspaper columns isn't much different from the first photographs ever taken of me by my father with his Kodak Brownie camera. I was round, I was bald, and I was not overly concerned about being photographed.

That first photograph ever taken of me was made in a small frame house across from the now-defunct Beulah-Hubbard school on a county road near the Newton County hamlet of Little Rock. The school had three hundred students in grades one through twelve, and my father was the principal there, while my mother was the English teacher and librarian.

In the photo, Sheila and I are propped up on pillows together. My father carried a copy of that photo in his wallet for as long as he lived. My mother's copy of it was kept in her Bible. Sheila was such a beautiful baby girl.

Our father, Leo Wilson Salter, was born November 29, 1913, in the Arlington community of Neshoba County on the family's one-hundred-acre farm. He was the eldest of five children.

He spoke often in later years of helping his parents "clear the new ground"—a euphemism for taking land from a wilderness condition to make it ready to grow crops. It was the hardest of labors, especially for a child, and those labors colored his work ethic for the rest of his life.

Dad worked constantly and worked hard. He refused to accept less from himself than his best and would accept no less from those around him. Despite a dry, wry sense of humor and a deep and abiding love for his family, my father was a man who measured others by the worth of their handshake as their bond and by their work ethics, and that included his own children.

A decorated U.S. Army Signal Corps combat veteran of the Normandy invasion on D-Day in 1944, my father received a "Dear John" letter from the woman he was dating when he shipped out for Europe. Her roommate felt sorry for Sgt. Salter and began a correspondence with him. Her name was Alline Haskins, and she would become my mother.

Our mother was born July 17, 1922, in the Townsend community in rural Kemper County. When she was five years old, her father would venture to the Mississippi Delta in Humphreys County to buy a farm in 1927. There was a mortgage against the farm at a Belzoni bank, secured by the land and to be paid by the proceeds of the crops.

That transaction and the subsequent spring planting barely preceded one of the major cataclysms in the history of Mississippi: the Great Flood of 1927. The flood washed my grandfather's crops away, along with his dreams and his property. In a single spring season, he lost everything he had save his family.

My mother was one of ten children. After the flood, my mom's family became sharecroppers in the Midnight community near Silver City in Humphreys County. My mother chopped cotton and picked cotton under the blazing Delta sun, pulling the staple crop from the stalks until her fingers bled. White sharecroppers worked alongside African American sharecroppers in a sea of cotton stalks. That was Mom's childhood.

The experience influenced my mother's attitude about race and class all of her life, and she would later try to teach her children toler-ance, kindness, and the evils of judging a person by anything less than their character.

Mom's keen mind allowed her to skip a few grades in school, and she graduated at the age of sixteen as the salutatorian of the twelve members of her Silver City High School Class of 1939. But she spent the next year working with her father in the cotton fields. Her future seemed as bleak as the Delta landscape. There simply was no money, and without money there appeared little chance of getting the educa-tion she believed would be her ticket out of the cotton fields and into a better life.

It was at that crossroads of my mother's life that she joined another family—a family that would provide the means for a poor Delta girl to pursue her dreams. My mom enrolled at Sunflower Junior College in Moorhead in the fall of 1940. As he had done for countless other Delta boys and girls, SJC president Paul West helped my mother find a job on campus working in the cafeteria that allowed her to work her way through school.

In 1942, Alline Haskins became the first of her family to graduate from college. Mom taught elementary school for a little while, but spent most of the war years working for Southern Bell as a telephone operator.

While teaching school in Kemper County after the war, she eventu-ally reunited with the soldier she'd written overseas, and in 1946 she married him. They were inseparable until the day he died forty-three years later.

Mom and Dad spent their lives teaching other people's children in the Mississippi public schools for a combined seventy-nine years. My sisters and I were always proud of them—proud of their grit and determination, proud of their courage and character, and proud of the values they imparted to us of personal integrity, tolerance, and compassion.

My older sister, Sharon S. Pratt, is a veteran educator and carries on the family tradition. She remains an important influence in my life even today.

From my father I learned the importance of standing one's ground. It was the hallmark value of his life—and as one can imagine, it produced a stubborn father who raised a stubborn son. I also credit my dad with teaching me that might doesn't always make right. During the critical years of school integration, my father stood up to the remnants of the Ku Klux Klan and the White Citizens' Council and did his best to ensure a peaceful integration of Neshoba Central and George Washington Carver high schools.

But my mother gave me the greatest gift—the love of reading and the desire to write. I make a living writing because of my mother's steady supply of books and her constant encouragement. Until Alzheimer's disease clouded her keen grammatical skills, she dutifully redlined my newspaper columns and brought my errors to my attention. She was always teaching right up to the end.

My twin sister and I parted company from a physical standpoint after completing our educations at Mississippi State University in the early 1980s. Sheila married and moved to Memphis. I married my college sweetheart and moved to Forest.

Over the next twenty-five years, we never lived closer than two hundred miles from each other and saw each other only a few times a year. But we called each other almost daily and the bond between us never diminished. She remained my best friend, my confidante, and my anchor to our shared past.

In 2005 our mother died after a long, slow decline. A month later my wife, Paula, died after a courageous twenty-two-year battle with multiple sclerosis. My daughter and I closed ranks and tried to move forward. It was a slow, painful process.

Sheila helped me through the fog of those losses, and, as it had been when we were children, there were times on the phone when all I could hear was the sound of her breathing, and yet that was enough.

Hurricane Katrina slammed into the Gulf Coast on August 29,

2005. After months of drifting, aimless grief, I plunged into my work and for the first time since my wife's death began to feel motivated to work, to write, and to live. I ventured to the coast amid the ruins and began to try to exhibit the compassion my mother had taught me with the courage my father had taught me to use in doing it.

A month after the storm I arrived home late one evening and sat down in an easy chair, exhausted from a visit to the disaster area. The phone rang. Somehow, I knew this call was bad news. My brother-in-law in Memphis was on the line, and he told me that Sheila was in the hospital and that I needed to come.

For the next hundred days I spent every spare moment away from work in Memphis trying to be close to my twin, to hear her breathing and to feel her weight against me when I would climb into the bed with her. We made that last journey together as her long, curly hair fell out, her sweet voice changed, and eventually her entire personality vanished into the oblivion of a stage 4 brain tumor. At the end, all that was left with us was her soul.

I spent the last week of her life with her and her husband in Memphis Baptist East. She chose to suspend any treatment at the end and to hold fast to her dignity. Sheila worked so hard all her life teaching her daughters how to live. At the end, it was her wish to teach them how to die—and she did.

Sheila was the repository of all my memories of a Mississippi childhood. When a twin tells you that a significant part of him dies when his other half dies, believe him. More than burying my parents, more even than burying my wife, Sheila's death rocked me to the core. I still struggle to make sense of her passing.

But when I come to that windswept hill in Memorial Park Cemetery in Memphis, I remember back to the sound of Sheila's breathing and the weight of her body against mine all those years ago in the crib and I am convinced that now—as then—she has merely fallen asleep before me and that I'm there to bear witness to her peaceful dreams until she awakens again.

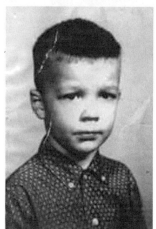

Wyatt Waters

Wyatt Waters, born in 1955, prepared all his life for a career as an artist. He holds B.A. and M.A. degrees from Mississippi College where he studied under Dr. Sam Gore. Wyatt and his wife Vicki own and operate Wyatt Waters Gallery in Olde Towne Clinton (www.wyattwaters.com). He has published two books of his own work and has illustrated many others. He has been the subject of articles *in American Artist, Art and Antiques*, and *Mississippi Magazine*. He has worked on many projects for public and corporate programs and is represented in many private, corporate, and museum collections.

The first thing I remember is moving to my new home in Florence, a small town just a few miles south of Jackson. My father moved us there from Wesson to take a coaching position with the high school. After moving into our new house, I remember my mother crying over how terrible the kitchen looked.

I walked with her to the Western Auto store where she bought some buckets of paint. She tacked flattened tin cans to the kitchen floor where there were holes and handed me a paint brush. We stood over the floor splattering different colored paints on the old flooring to create faux linoleum.

I claimed the Naugahyde-covered wooden desk in the family room as my own. It was specifically turned to face directly away from the TV and immediately behind my father's chair. The desk was full of useless stationery that had been left behind by the school's old coach. I was incredibly happy now that I had something I wouldn't get in trouble for drawing on, and I drew continuously as my father watched television behind me.

My mother walked me to the community center where Mrs. Rose Taylor held summer classes for local kids. Given Mrs. Taylor's interest in art, her classes were decidedly slanted toward the visual. She read us stories and then had us draw pictures about the story. I loved that.

I think I may have started drawing simply because I was bored. My mother, whose father was an artist, noticed that I scribbled on every available surface, and she began to save bits and pieces of paper for me to use. My favorite was the cardboard insert that a new shirt just off the shelf of the store was wrapped around. It was sturdy and white and a convenient size.

When I was six, my mother marched me down to Miss Rose's house with a special request. We stood at her back door in the rain and asked Miss Rose to give me art lessons. She told us she could not do that. She had never in her life taught art.

So we went back home, and before we could get into dry clothes, Miss Rose was calling to say she would give it a try.

Miss Rose gave me my most important education in art, and her lessons continued through elementary school. She taught me how to work from life, and she showed me how to recognize the way colors change against each other, and how to look for the direction of the light, and to notice the way light and shadow came together to describe form—all lessons that I use to this day.

She also taught me, more than anything else, a love of art; and she told me with conviction that I *would* be an artist and have a studio of my own. That was always what I planned for my life.

In school, drawing and daydreaming were my favorite pastimes. I had a best friend who joined me in these adventures and together we plotted and planned all sorts of inventions which I would transfer to visual images on paper—the blueprints of our dreams. This teamwork lasted throughout our high school years.

Once our teacher read us a story called "Little Black, a Pony" and asked us to illustrate it. This was right up my alley, and since our house was next door to a pasture with horses, I had live models to

draw. I proudly took my portrait of a horse family to school—an ana-
tomically correct stallion and a mother nursing her colt. The teacher
pinned every picture up on the bulletin board—except mine. Many
years later that teacher brought my portrait of the horse family into
my studio and gave it to me. She had saved it all those years, even
though she felt it was too "realistic" to display in the classroom.

When I was in sixth grade, I broke my leg playing football and had
to go to school in a wheelchair. At that time I developed another lasting interest. I learned to play the guitar. I didn't have a guitar, mind
you, but I made a photocopy of an instruction book, and I drew frets
and strings on a piece of cardboard, and so I knew chord forms before
I ever heard them.

At my mother's instigation, my father the football coach huddled
with Ernie Workman the band director and found me a Regal guitar,
which Dad bought for five dollars. In my junior high years, I formed
a band with a friend and wrote music and sang my songs.

My family moved to Clinton when I was in the tenth grade. This
was a big move to a big school. I left behind Miss Rose, and I left my
first girlfriend. The high school years at Clinton High were generally
uneventful. Though I shunned all the art classes, to this day school-
mates come up to me and say, "I remember you from art class. I always knew you'd make it."

After high school graduation, I enrolled at Mississippi College,
where Mr. Ron Alexander, my faculty advisor, suggested I choose
another career besides art. I think my high school years had erod-
ed the confidence to make the commitment I needed. I am forever
grateful for the honesty that motivated me to change. Around that
same time Dr. Sam Gore came into my life and gave me the encouragement I needed to make art my major study. He gave me a
work study job which turned out to be more of an apprenticeship.
For the next four years the art department was my second home.

I received a bachelor's degree in art with a minor in English and
received the Bellamann Award for Art and Creative Writing. I imme-

diately returned to graduate school at MC where Dr. Gore arranged a work/study assistantship for me. He gave me a practical education working from life and a strong background in design. Writing my master's thesis forced me to explore the physics of light and color perception in a way that otherwise I would never have done. This informed and focused my work and changed the way I painted.

By the time I got my master's, I was selling paintings at flea markets and art fairs on weekends and beginning a new phase of my education—marketing. I would set up my easel at a street fair and do fifteen-minute pencil portraits of passersby for $7.50 a pop. All manner of people stopped and visited. On a table behind me, I'd have a stack of my paintings to show just in case someone asked. In this way I met museum and gallery directors as well as fellow artists.

My shyness was broken down and chipped away by these experiences. I still have friends and clients from those early days.

I won't forget those days—the teachers, the friends, the helping hands of the arts community—and the valuable lessons learned. They taught me to never doubt my feelings and to steadfastly trust my instincts.

Gwendolyn Gong

Gwendolyn Gong, born in the Mississippi Delta in 1954, received B.A. and M.A. degrees from the University of Mississippi and her Ph.D. from Purdue. She taught for fourteen years at Texas A&M. In 1995 Dr. Gong moved to Hong Kong where she is professor of English at the Chinese University of Hong Kong. She is co-author of *Editing: The Design of Rhetoric, A Writer's Repertoire*, and *A Reader's Repertoire*, and is the founding editor of the *Asian Journal of English Language Teaching*.

If you drive down Highway 61 south past Cleveland, you'll pass the Katfish Korral and approach Bellazar's restaurant, where you'll turn onto Highway 446, going west. Down that stretch of road lies Boyle, my hometown. Cross the bayou bridge, and keep your eye out for an expanse of concrete—a barren lot. This large empty space, occupying about two-thirds of the town block, was where my daddy's store once stood.

K. W. Gong & Co. was the name of our family business, a general store that reflected my father's ideas about the world. Daddy held that everything—from groceries to dry goods—had its place and purpose. The overall layout of the store's four walls was strategic, and every item needed to be thoughtfully organized according to aisle and shelf.

Along the front wall, lined by large untinted windows, Daddy positioned long freezers and refrigerators that contained items our patrons frequently requested: milk, eggs, prepackaged meats, frozen vegetables, TV dinners, pizzas, and ice cream. He believed that the "cold" items somehow neutralized the hot sunshine that beamed through the large windowpanes; the coolers also served as a pseudo wall that burglars would have to get past should they try a nighttime break-in.

Opposite the front wall, Daddy placed two more freezers, full of hens, ducks, fish, chitterlings, oxtails, roasts, and pork ribs. On the other side of the freezers, he placed kegs of loose nails and staples that we sold by the pound. In addition, he lined the back wall with household items such as dishwashing powders, bath soaps, scrubbing pads, drain cleaners, bathroom tissue, and insecticides. These were items that had strong smells and that customers did not routinely buy every time they came to the store.

The side walls of the store were logical extensions of Daddy's mind, too. Near the back, the right-hand wall featured canned goods—coffee, fruits, vegetables, evaporated milk—as well as boxed goods, such as tea, oatmeal, and grits. The front of the right side wall housed a large cooler full of fresh vegetables: greens, carrots, beets, rutabagas, cabbages, and the like. Daddy was adamant that perishables should be arranged near the front of the store so that we could "push" them and monitor them for freshness. Consequently, the left side wall was lined with coolers full of wax-covered cheese wheels, "sticks" of sandwich meats, whole chickens, ground beef, pork loins, slab bacon, salted fatback, and link sausages that we would package for customers upon request. Beside these meat coolers were two adding machines atop a long checkout counter wide enough to accommodate two customers at a time. And behind this counter were tobacco products, medicines, toothpastes, shoe polish, penny candies, shaving cream, razor blades, and hardware supplies.

Every aisle within these store "walls" was likewise planned and stocked according to each item's shelf life, customer demand, size, smell, and type. In arranging the store, Daddy kept in mind what kind of goods we offered and what kinds of customers frequented our business. Daddy's way of envisioning products and consumer needs resulted in a consistent logic for everything that provided a mental map our patrons could use to figure out the location of any item in the store. Everything had its place.

This orderly "universe" was my first schoolhouse, where my parents served as my most valuable teachers. They tutored me in academic subjects as well as cultural and family values. In more indirect ways, they taught by example, showing me the power of learning by observing others; for in many ways, that is how my parents gained knowledge about people, places, and things in our little Delta town. I witnessed how they interacted with customers, experienced other cultures, and negotiated their cultural place as Mississippi Chinese between the black and white majority groups. The store was the vehicle that enabled my family to create their own sense of place in Boyle. As Daddy firmly believed, everything and everybody have their place and purpose; and we had ours.

While neither Mama nor Daddy had much formal schooling, they believed mightily in education and relished occasions when they could transmit what they knew to their children. This was especially true when I was in grammar school. They helped me with homework and explained ideas that I had particular trouble grasping.

For example, I recall a time when I was in second grade and couldn't get the hang of fractions. Daddy gathered handfuls of oranges and apples, directing me to follow him to the kitchen, located at the back of the store, connecting our business to our living quarters. There, the fruit tumbled onto the oil cloth–covered table. I scrambled to steady the red and orange objects while Daddy retrieved a paring knife and took a seat beside me. "See this apple?" he asked. "It's a *whole* apple." Then he sliced the Red Delicious in two, four, six, and eight pieces—each time stopping to explain the relationship between the wedges and fractions. After he had illustrated different fractions and there were no more uncut apples, it was my turn: Daddy had me explain fractions to him, using the thick-skinned navel oranges before me. Our reward came at the end of the math lesson; he and I sat together, snacking on wedges of all dimensions. From moments like this one, I felt a special bond with my daddy, a simple yet meaningful instance when Daddy made time for me, turning his attention from the store to teach me a lesson that also made me feel important.

Mama was all business when she tutored me. She'd read out lists of spelling words and quiz me on times tables. These lessons were typically held after dinner before our nightly chores, a time when business was slow. Multitasking, Mama called out words or multiplication problems, rang up goods, collected payments, and sacked groceries, in a seamless series of movements. I sat nearby on a folding chair, rocking back and forth, spinning a five-foot candy rack around on its base, as I responded to the prompts with strings of letters and numbers. Spelling came easy to me, but "mental math" (memorizing and reciting multiplication tables) was a challenge. Mama seemed to realize this, and so she expeditiously ran through the spelling lists that I enjoyed, leaving her more time to drill me on the "dreaded" times tables. She had an uncanny way of remembering which problems I missed or hesitated on, and it was these equations that she fired back at me—a real-life, oral flash card. After these sessions under Mama's stern and watchful eye, I actually looked forward to my nightly chores!

Education was important and went hand in hand with hard work, responsibility, and family. The store required that we were open six and a half days, from 6 a.m. to 9:30 p.m. or later. Daddy reminded us that the "public" depended on us, expected us to be open when folks needed things. And he hated to miss making a sale, so he did his best to keep long and regular store hours.

As was the case in Chinese family stores in the Delta, everyone worked. I was the youngest of seven children. My oldest three sisters had finished university, married, and moved from the Delta, and my older brother was studying at Ole Miss by the time I was a regular worker in the store. So that left my teenaged siblings—Patricia Mae and Stephen—and me to continue the tradition of doing chores in the store.

Instead of participating in after-school activities, Pat, Stephen, and I would come home and sit behind the checkout counter, doing our homework while minding the store. We ate dinner in shifts, allowing some to eat while others worked at the counter. At night, we had our different tasks. Mama manned the counter while Daddy cleaned the meat slicer, restocked the shelves, and inspected perishables to cull rotten fruit and vegetables. We children took turns sweeping the store, filling the soft drink and beer cases, sorting empty soft drink bottles, stocking the cigarette racks, and burning the trash. Most everything in our daily lives—eating, working, studying—revolved around the business and our responsibilities. We were a team and we developed a sense of family loyalty and cultural identity from our work in the store.

Many children may not know what their parents do at work. That was not the case for my siblings and me. We worked in the store as soon as we learned to count money. Working alongside Mama and Daddy, we always understood, firsthand, the importance of a strong work ethic. Daddy had a plaque in his office that read, "Nobody owes you a living. You have to earn it." And so our parents toiled and brought us up "knowing" work.

While Mama and Daddy taught me through direct interaction in the store, they also shaped my thinking in a more indirect way: through their interaction with customers.

For Daddy, the best instances had to do with his favorite pastime: fishing. He was a fisherman of the first order. He knew the simple pleasure a person could experience in the act of fishing. Daddy owned several boats and motors, and gobs of fishing paraphernalia. We sold fishing stuff at the store: hooks, line, lead, tackles, and such. Daddy would open the store early in the morning, hoping that fishermen going out to the lake would stop at the store to pick up fishing supplies and food. He'd encourage them to stop back by on their way home; and they did. Then he'd sell these fellows some more provisions and get them to tell their fish stories. This apparently simple act had a complex purpose: it provided Daddy with reconnaissance, information that he'd either pass along to other fishermen the next morning, or that he'd benefit from if he were lucky enough to get out to the lake himself. Daddy, a lake, a motorboat, a fishing pole, and some bait. What more could a person want on a clear day? Though I never learned to love fishing, I did appreciate the power of having personal passions for nonwork pursuits. And I discovered the social and practical value of interacting with customers.

Mama also had a way with customers. Her modus operandi had to do with food rather than fishing. There were always great aromas from Mama's kitchen that wafted into the store. Daddy said that Mama's cooking was good for business, for it made folks hungry and want to buy more groceries.

I suppose you could say that the kitchen was an extension of the store. In a way, the kitchen was the cultural "bridge" between our Asian world and the southern world of Caucasians and African Americans. For it was in our kitchen that Mama prepared dishes from recipes she learned when she was a schoolgirl in Canton, China; and it was in this same kitchen that Mama learned sumptuous Deep South cooking.

In the store, Mama would chat with customers as she totaled their bills and sacked their items. While customers were paying, Mama would casually ask what they were planning to make with the ingredients they were buying. If the ingredients were for some dish that Mama already knew how to make, she'd hand over the person's change directly. However, if these items were going to be used to make foods that Mama didn't know how to make or wanted another variation of, she'd slowly hand over the customer's change, lean over the counter and continue the conversation by asking more about that recipe. If the patron had time, Mama would escort him or her around the store, gathering the ingredients needed to make that particular dish. Then, she'd invite the customer into our kitchen to show her how to make it—right then and there.

That was how Mama learned to cook southern. After the customer left, she'd write down what she could remember; then, she'd go over to her rack of cookbooks and compare her version to published ones. From that point, she would make these dishes from her memory, cryptic notes and sketches, and senses.

Mama had many strategies for discovering how to prepare southern cuisine. She learned by watching, interviewing, note taking, drawing, listening, tasting, smelling, feeling, reading, and doing. She also learned by sharing what she had cooked with other people. Like Daddy, Mama learned from customers by engaging them in conversation and being genuinely curious about them, their food, and their culture. And she shared her gleanings with us all.

My parents, my greatest teachers, are gone now. The store is gone as well. All that remains are memories of my Mississippi childhood in the store and of my parents and the education they gave me. From their lessons and by their example, they created for me a stable sense of place, purpose, values, identity, and belonging, situated amid the increasingly complex racial, sociocultural, educational, and political milieu of the Delta in the 1960s and 1970s. They gave me a sense of how I could make a space for myself as a Mississippi Chinese—lessons that live on within me though my schoolhouse and teachers are no more.

Maggie Wade Dixon

Maggie Wade Dixon, born in Crystal Springs in 1960, graduated from Utica High School and attended Jackson State. After transferring to Mississippi College, she began her broadcasting career in the school radio station and later worked at WJDX-MISS 103. She was hired at WLBT-TV in her senior year and since then has worked as a weather anchor, market researcher, weekend news anchor, and currently as weekday evening anchor. She has appeared in two feature films. She has received more than four hundred awards for her contributions, including recognition from the U.S. Congress for her work with foster children.

I don't remember a time when God didn't have his hand on my life and the lives of my sisters and brothers. I remember almost drowning, and my brother, who couldn't swim either, pulled me and our cousin out of the water just in time. I remember swinging from trees like we had seen in the movies and were convinced we could do, too. And our walks through the woods! I think I have seen every animal native to Mississippi, except maybe alligators. The only thing about my childhood that bothers me is this: I didn't take time to enjoy it.

I was too busy trying to grow up, and I was questioning God about why he put me on this farm in Crystal Springs. I was convinced that Diahann Carroll was my mother and God had made a mistake and put me in the wrong place.

Thank God for his wisdom and mercy. I can see now that he put me exactly where I should have been, and he blessed me with a wonderful family to grow up with—a mom and dad, three sisters and three brothers, and then a husband and children and now a new son-in-law. I am very fortunate to have been surrounded by aunts and uncles and many, many cousins. All four of my grandparents lived close by so I saw them almost every day.

My Big Daddy, Walter Wade, Sr., was a character, a prankster with a capital P. I remember being five years old and he would teach us dirty jokes and tell us it was poetry and to go and show our mama what we learned. We got in so much trouble. One day my sister Lorna and I got back at him. When he went to sleep we put braids all over his hair and clipped them with our barrettes. He woke up and chased us all over the house, laughing all the while.

Lorna and I were only fourteen months apart. We always dressed alike and people thought we were twins. We did everything together. Her battles were mine and my battles were hers.

My grandmother, called Big Mama, was an amazing woman. Blind for much of my childhood, she knew each and every one of the grand-children who lived around her on the farm. I asked her how she always knew us apart and she said, "By the way you smell and the sound of your voices." She cooked for herself and was independent. She was always my saving grace. I could run to her for anything. I am named Magnolia after her. And they say they gave me that name because I was as beautiful as the flower and as strong as the tree. Certainly that description fit my grandmother. She always told us stories, my favorite being how she eloped from the church choir to marry Big Daddy. He laughed and said he was a baby and she kidnapped him from his crib.

My mother's parents lived about fifteen miles from us. We visited them every Sunday. One time my grandmother invited the whole family to a big holiday dinner. When I went into the dining room and saw the table groaning under the many dishes, I became hysterical. The centerpiece of the meal, a small pink animal with an apple in his mouth, was staring straight at me. Nobody could convince me that she hadn't cooked her dog and served him up for our dinner.

We got up early on Sunday for church and Sunday school. There were no excuses. Often we went to services at several churches, and no matter how long the day was, we knew not to complain. Summertime meant revival at the churches. If it was hot my uncle would sell sno-cones out under the trees, and if it was cool, there might be boiled peanuts.

When school was out for the summer vacation, the days were ours. Lorna and I made playhouses outside. We got many spankings for taking Mama's "good stuff" out of the house to our playhouses. We set tables with tea sets and brought out our dolls. When our cousin came from next door and ransacked our playhouse, Lorna would take him on while I sat and cried. I was the tender-hearted one, afraid of my shadow.

I didn't like horror movies, and I still don't. Every day after school Lorna insisted on watching *Dark Shadows*. I hated the show; I hated the music; I hated all the evil characters. One night when my parents were next door at our uncle's house, we kids, having the house to ourselves, went a little wild. We did not hear Dad when he came home and found us jumping on the beds having a pillow fight. He decided to teach us a lesson. All of a sudden we heard the squeaky screen door open, we heard footsteps; we saw a reflection in the mirror: a man with his collar turned up creeping up the hall. I burst out crying, but brave Lorna got a broom and shouted all sorts of threats. The figure retreated. We heard the door close softly. My mother was furious when we told her about our mysterious visitor. She knew it was our father and lit into him for scaring us children. My dad just laughed and said, "They stopped jumping on the bed, didn't they?"

My favorite times when school was out in summer were spent with Lorna. We would put on our hats and go looking for blackberries, blueberries, plums, and muscadines. Mama would make cobblers out of the fruit we brought home.

Once my cousin Roy, Lorna, and I got into trouble when we went to the woods looking for a tree with a honeycomb. We found one about two miles from the house. We'd brought everything we needed to smoke out the bees so that we could get the honey. We set the fire and then put it out and got the smoke we needed, but we were soon trapped by the bees. We huddled down and hid to wait out the bees. Hours later, it was getting dark and the tree began to burn. By this time, the family was looking for us. My dad saw the smoke curling in the sky, and he and Uncle Paul followed it and rescued us from the bees and led us back home.

Kids don't have that kind of childhood anymore. They don't get to have those adventures with their families. I would never let my children just roam off into the woods. It isn't safe now. In my childhood, every grown-up in our community kept an eye out for the children. We were allowed to be kids, to explore, to feel free, and to learn. Those were the good old days, filled with faith, love, and family.

Yes, God has always had his hand on my life and angels on my path. I am truly blessed. And now I'm old enough to know that, even if I could, I wouldn't change one thing.

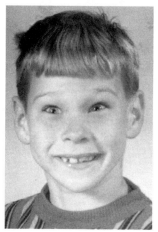

Robert St. John

Robert St. John, born in 1961 in Hattiesburg, is the executive chef and owner of the Purple Parrot Café and Crescent City Grill in Hattiesburg and Meridian, Mississippi. He writes a weekly syndicated food and humor column and has published seven books with such notable publishers as Hyperion and Rutledge Hill Press. St. John has been featured on the Food Network, Turner South, and the Travel Channel. His credits are now growing to include television projects and a full line of gourmet foods.

It was a time before reality TV, before Watergate, and Contragate, and *Frontgate*. The cold war was in full bloom, Jimi Hendrix was alive, and the Beatles were still together. Captain America had morphed from a World War II comic book superhero with a star-spangled shield into a counterculture icon on a Harley-Davidson. Dr. King and Bobby Kennedy were gone, but Jim Crow was still here. Elvis was alive, skinny even, and only went to Vegas to get married. It was a time before AIDS and low-carb diets, and New Orleans was still the city that care forgot. Television had Carson and Cronkite and Little Joe Cartwright. A war was being lost, and a cultural shift was occurring, though Berkeley and Kent State were light years away. Hair was long and days were longer. Doors were left unlocked, and I knew every dog in the neighborhood.

The Hillendale subdivision of Hattiesburg, Mississippi, was being constructed as the babies boomed. It was filled with the low-rate mortgages of Depression-born parents and the tall pines native to my corner of the South. Hillendale stretched from Howlin' Wolf's Highway 49 on the east to Eisenhower's Interstate 59 on the west. My mother, brother, and I moved into a small house on a small lot midway between those two roads in 1968.

There were two-car garages, no sidewalks, and homes filled with discernment and dysfunction. Children spent summers on bikes, in creeks, and wrestling on St. Augustine grass.

Neighborhood boys ran alongside dogs while squeezing every ounce of sunlight out of the long summer days. Appetites were earned. My love for food and my love for dogs were shaped and solidified in the same moment and the same place.

The ladies of my neighborhood were brilliant cooks. They prided themselves on the dishes they prepared. There were no micro greens or infused vinegars, no baby vegetables or precooked entrees. Everything was made from scratch, simple, honest, pure. Families sat together at the same table—television off—and shared a meal. A mother called her children to supper and they ran to the table.

The third meal of the day was always called "supper." The term "dinner" was reserved for a more formal midday meal. In earlier decades, the call to supper had been a whistle, not a metal coach's whistle, but sweet airy birdlike notes from the pursed lips of a woman who was too polite to scream her son's name from the front porch. Each mother had a different style and tune. Fifty years later, my friend Bill can replicate, to an exact note, the whistle of his mother. The birdlike change in pitch and tenor of a mother's whistle can bring a tear to the eye of the grown man who recalls it. The birdcall whistle was unassuming and sedate, like the decades that spawned it.

The call to supper in the late 1960s and early 1970s was different. In my neighborhood most mothers had a bell. The bell was the clarion call for supper. Every bell had a different tone and each could be heard from blocks away. Most bells were of the come-and-get-it handheld variety, no larger than a mayonnaise jar.

In the early evening, just before dusk, as the asphalt started to cool, bells could be heard from back doors and back porches in all directions. The neighborhood became a sporadic symphony of chimes—the mother's opus, an unorganized and unintentional hand-bell ensemble. In the middle of a heated Wiffle ball game, a bell would ring from blocks away, and the conversation would go something like this: "Pat, that's your bell. See you tomorrow." "No, that's Stan's bell." "No, it's Robby's bell. His little brother broke their old one and his mom got a new one."

"That's my bell, guys; I gotta get home for supper."

Every boy knew the sound of his mother's bell. My mother—a devout disciple of all things Early American—opted for a miniature version of the Liberty Bell, minus the crack. She purchased it on a Colonial Dames field trip to Williamsburg. It had a Williamsburg yellow handle and rang long and true, with a deeper tone than all of the others. And when it rang, I ran.

A friend whose dad kept a large boat on the Gulf Coast was called home to the sound of an air horn that could be heard all the way to Eisenhower's interstate. The mother of another friend who had recently moved into town used a cowbell.

Most boys had a bell; Ernest had Cokie. Cokie was an elderly black woman who had moved down from a Mississippi Delta plantation when Ernest's mother married into the neighborhood. She lived in a converted garage and served as the family's nanny, cook, maid, babysitter, and town crier. While other mothers were ringing bells, Cokie walked up and down the pine-lined streets yelling, "Ernest. Ernest." After ten minutes and a few blocks, the cry changed to a more longing, "Ernest, come home!" If we quietly moved from street to street, avoiding Cokie's detection, we could usually elicit a remark such as, "Ernest, get your little white ass home! Supper's getting cold!"

Occasionally when bells didn't get the job done, mothers would drive around the neighborhood—a scotch and water in one hand, the steering wheel of the Vista Cruiser station wagon in the other— playing an ever-moving game of cat and mouse–style hide and seek. The mother, an unwilling participant in the game, bellowed her son's name as she slowly drove from block to block one step behind the group.

Just as I knew everyone's bell, I knew everyone's dog. It was a time

192 ROBERT ST. JOHN

before leash laws and pooper scoopers, and the dogs of my neighbor-hood—like the kids of the day—ran free and with abandon. William Dunlap says, "Some civilizations worship dogs, some work them, others put them on the menu." Hillendale fell into the first category.

The dogs of my neighborhood were more like those of a commune than pets of individual houses or owners. I belonged to the neighbor-hood and all the dogs belonged to me.

Buffy and Sue—a cocker spaniel and an English setter—lived in my house. Lucky lived across the street and was a mixed breed with one blue eye and a limp. Scooter was a dachshund. Cappy was a cock-er, too, named after his owner, Cathy. Cola was a poodle named after her seller.

Sam and Caesar were black labs who lived one block apart. Caesar was the neighborhood Don Juan and prone to random bouts of leg humping. He is primarily responsible for being the first, and only, time I ever saw a romance broken up by a garden hose. Sam, on the other hand, kept his love life to himself.

There were Festus, and Rastus, and Rufus—all mutts—and Frank, a golden retriever that would fetch a stick out of the lake until your arm got so tired you could no longer throw.

Son was a trembling Chihuahua with a vicious growl, and Frosty was an Eskimo spitz who once bit my face when I sat on his tail. Dy-namite was a poodle, Bijou was an Afghan, and Piper was an inces-santly yapping terrier. Bertha Butt was a small mutt I found and gave to the wife of a preacher, and Sheba was an English sheepdog who al-ways seemed miserable living in the heat and humidity of south Mis-sissippi. At one or more times in my life, I befriended all of them.

Willie Morris once wrote, "The dog of your boyhood teaches you a great deal about friendship, and love, and death." I believe that the neighborhood dogs taught me and my friends how to live together and how to interact with one another, through fights, and breakups, and times we felt lost or alone. They taught us the virtues of loyalty within friendship and gave us an early glimpse into pain and loss and unrequited love. They ran all day long, and like us, they ran with purpose when they were called home.

Today a mother calls "supper" and kids run—not to a table—but to a minivan. Soccer has replaced Wiffle ball and cell phones have replaced bells. I still live within eight blocks of the small house on the small lot. I don't know the dogs in my neighborhood. I don't know my neighbors, and I am ashamed that I never took the time to learn Cokie's full name.

The dusk of my youth was filled with barks and bells. As the sun set on my neighborhood, a carillon rang through the streets. The clangs were interrupted by the occasional bleat of a boat horn, clank of a cowbell, or the frustrated cry of a housekeeper. Birds fell silent as smoke from backyard barbeques dissipated and televisions were tuned to *Mannix* and *Hawaii Five-O*. One by one the bells surrendered to crickets and bullfrogs, as darkness fell on Hillendale.

Jerry Rice

Jerry Rice, a Mississippi Valley State graduate, was born in 1962 in the Delta town of Crawford. He is widely regarded as the greatest wide receiver in NFL history. As a San Francisco 49er, he won three Super Bowl rings. He was chosen for the Pro Bowl team thirteen times and All-Pro ten times. He also played for the Oakland Raiders, where he was part of an AFC championship team, and the Seattle Seahawks, a Division Championship team. He retired from football in 2006 and was inducted into the Mississippi Sports Hall of Fame in 2007. He lives in the Bay area with his wife and two children.

One day in early September of my sophomore year of high school, 1978, I decided to play hooky with a friend, despite the fear of getting caught and whipped by my father. We snuck out of class to make our way off campus. Suddenly, the school principal, Mr. Ezell Wickes, spotted us. He and I made eye contact before we bolted. Mr. Wickes never caught up to us but seeing that this was a small school, he easily recognized my face and clothing. Suffice it to say, I knew what I had coming when I returned. He had a big old leather strap in his office and he gave me five hard hits with it. It was painful.

But Mr. Wickes witnessed how fast I had sprinted away from him, and realized my speed could be put to good use to keep me out of trouble. So he forced me to meet with Charles Davis, the head football coach at B. L. Moor High School. After an initial conversation between us, him doing most of the talking, he convinced me to try out for the football team. My mother was against it initially, as she was concerned about my body, and she also knew that my shyness might be a liability in such a rough game—shyness in that I didn't like confrontation and never seemed very aggressive. (And she thought basketball was my future, anyway.) As for my father, he seemed indifferent, more concerned with bricklaying and providing for the family. My older brother Tom was already a high school football star so it wasn't that my parents didn't know what the sport was all about—the violent hits, the summer workouts, the emphasis on football from local townspeople, as it was *the* thing to do on Friday nights. As for me, if I was going to play, it wasn't good enough just to be average. I had to be great. The only way I knew how to do anything was to outwork, outperform, and outplay everyone else. Even though my father wasn't watching, I felt he was, and I didn't want to disappoint him.

Coach Davis knew when to be tough but also when to show compassion. I immediately took a liking to him as tryouts began. I wasn't scared, though I knew the other guys had an advantage over me because they had played organized football before. I wanted the guys to accept me. The best way I thought I could do that was to work hard and get good—fast.

It took me a while to learn the game of football. I watched the older guys on the team and copied how they practiced and how they played. Not only was I still impressed by the little quarterback, Kent Thomas, but I idolized Lester Tate, a bulky running back who had speed and grace. He was the man on the field and popular in the school hallways.

Both Kent and Lester had style. They had something in their attitude that personified confidence. It wasn't arrogance; it was a complete presentation of how they looked, how they practiced, and how they approached every game. Presentation is everything and it's something that I have lived by every day since.

The high school team practiced and played on a field that was more dirt than grass, surrounded by barely a hundred seats with stadium lights on one side. The helmets and pads and uniforms were in poor condition. The upperclassmen and starters got the "best" equipment, and by best I mean the least torn up. Pants, shoes, and socks were all in very limited supply. Not having much only made me want more. If there was money in the school to spend, and there wasn't much, it tended to go toward things like books and classroom materials.

I worked hard in tryouts and was fortunate enough to make the team as a tenth grader, despite my rookie tendencies, like running the wrong route, dropping easy balls, and even putting on my pads the wrong way. When it came to the season, though, I played sparingly as a kick returner and, occasionally, as a defensive back and receiver. Because of my size, lanky build, good hands, and speed, returning kicks and playing receiver and defensive back seemed like a good fit. Speed was necessary to be a running back, but at six foot one, I was just too tall and I certainly didn't know enough about the game to be a quarterback. I didn't quite have the game or the techniques down, but I was in great condition. True to form, after a tough practice I would run the ten miles or so back home.

Coach Davis used to run us up and down hills every day after practice as either a form of conditioning or punishment, forty yards up, and forty yards down. Guys would be throwing up on the way up *and* down. I remember after practice one day I decided to run some more hills to get in better condition on my own. I started up the slope, sweating profusely in the hot August sun of Mississippi, and said, "I give up." I was so tired and hot I walked back down the hill and headed to the locker room to hang it up for the day. But then the voices in my head started to talk. "Never quit!" I kept hearing it over and over again. I stopped walking, turned around, and started running the hills again.

Before the following season, my junior year, I knew what I needed to do to get better; I worked hard in the off season to get faster and stronger. I watched the upperclassmen as I waited for my opportunity. Some summer days I would be up at dawn, work all day long with my father and brothers laying brick, get dropped off at school for practice, and then have to run the ten miles home because I had no ride.

The run home was often in pitch darkness and the route took me along woods. It was silent and dark and the littlest sounds from the woods scared me to death. So I picked up my pace.

I had to be the best and had to prove myself to Coach Davis and to my teammates. Maybe that came from always wanting to please my father. As a result, my junior year was my breakout season. I focused on playing receiver and defensive back, and playing one position helped me play the other better. I learned how to run routes and how to cover, how to receive and how to intercept, but mostly, I just relied on instinct and reacted to my opponent. Our team won games and I started to shine on the field, scoring touchdowns and smothering opponents on defense.

I was still very shy, avoiding crowds and girls, and I only had one or two buddies with whom I occasionally hung out. I was comfortable as a loner and didn't let anyone get close to me. I was so used to being alone that it was comforting to me just to be on my own. (I still am somewhat of a loner today.) But classmates and teachers started to notice me more, as I became more of a leader and star on the football field. I have to admit, it was nice to have classmates approach me and say, "Good job" after a Friday game. But it wasn't satisfying for me the way I had hoped. I thought if I excelled on the field and gained recognition from classmates, it would make me feel whole. I was wrong. I did like being part of a team, as it allowed me to feel that I fit in somewhere, but a big piece of me still felt like a loner. My parents were supportive of my game and efforts, and always tried to be there for every game, though my mother cringed every time I took a lick on the field, something she never got used to.

Though my stardom blossomed, and I came to love playing football, I did give other sports a try, competing in the high jump on the track team and playing forward on the Moor High School basketball team. I wasn't a typical high jumper who approached the bar, twisted, and turned my body before leaping backward over the bar and landing on my back. No, I just leapt and straddled the bar, landing on my feet. My first year on the track team, one of our stars was entered in so many events, our coach replaced him with me in the anchor leg of the team relay. For those of you not familiar with a track relay, each team has four runners, and each runner runs one lap around the track after being passed a baton from a teammate. Typically, the fastest runner runs the last or anchor lap. Well, on this particular day in the late 1970s, I was the anchor runner and was handed the baton with about a twenty to thirty yard lead on the closest team. I was home free! I bolted out and burned out. I got sucked up by the runner behind me who blew past and won the race for his team. After I crossed the finish line, I remember collapsing onto my knees, dehydrated and exhausted. I had let my team down and failed.

It took me many more years to recognize that I couldn't win at everything. Abraham Lincoln lost elections before becoming our great president. Henry Ford went bankrupt before creating the automobile empire that bears his name. Babe Ruth failed to get a hit the majority of times he came to the plate. Michael Jordan missed twice as many shots as he made. If those at the top of their profession don't win in everything all the time, I think it's safe to say that neither will we.

Acknowledgments

The editors are deeply indebted to the writers represented in this collection who responded promptly to our various requests and paused in their extremely busy schedules to reflect, reach back in time and retrieve, shape into words, and then share their stories about growing up in Mississippi and about memorable influences in their lives. In addition, we thank Craig Gill at University Press of Mississippi for his excellent counsel and guidance with this project, and we wish to gratefully acknowledge the generous assistance we received from Bill Kehoe, a gentleman, a true friend, and always a lover of good books. Finally, we thank James Patterson at 119 Gallery for his support and advice, his calming encouragement, and his expert help in all things pertaining to photography.

Copyright Acknowledgments and Photography credits

Elizabeth Spencer
      From *Landscapes of the Heart: A Memoir* by Elizabeth Spencer
      Copyright © 1997 by Elizabeth Spencer
      Reprinted by permission of Random House, Inc.
Ellen Douglas
      From *Truth: Four Stories I Am Finally Old Enough to Tell* by Ellen Douglas
      Copyright © 1998 by Ellen Douglas
      Reprinted by permission of Algonquin Books of Chapel Hill
B. B. King
      Excerpt from pp. 21–26 from *Blues All Around Me: The Autobiography of B. B. King*
         by B. B. King with David Ritz
      Copyright © 1997 by B. B. King
      Reprinted by permission of HarperCollins Publishers

Jim Weatherly
"Misty Mississippi Morning"
Copyright © by Jim Weatherly
Reprinted by permission of Universal Music Publishing
Noel Polk
From "I. J." in *The Southern Quarterly* 40, no. 3 (Spring 2002): 181–86 by Noel Polk
Copyright © 2002 by Noel Polk
Reprinted by permission of *The Southern Quarterly* and Noel Polk
Jimmy Buffett
From *A Pirate Looks at Fifty* by Jimmy Buffett
Copyright © 1998 by Jimmy Buffett
Reprinted by permission of Random House, Inc.
Clifton L. Taulbert
"Flood of 2005 Joins Flood of '27 in Memories" by Clifton Taulbert
Copyright © 2006 by Clifton Taulbert
First Printing in the *Clarion-Ledger* 2006
Reprinted by permission of Clifton Taulbert
Edward Cohen
From *The Peddler's Grandson: Growing Up Jewish in Mississippi*
    by Edward Cohen
Copyright © 1999 by Edward Cohen
Reprinted by permission of University Press of Mississippi
Lorian Hemingway
From *Walk on Water: A Memoir* by Lorian Hemingway
Copyright © 1998 by Lorian Hemingway
Reprinted by permission of Simon & Schuster Adult Publishing Group
Sela Ward
From pp. 30–35 from *Homesick: A Memoir* by Sela Ward
Copyright © 2002 by Sela Ward
Reprinted by permission of HarperCollins Publishers
W. Ralph Eubanks
From *Ever Is a Long Time: A Journey into Mississippi's Dark Past, A Memoir* by
    W. Ralph Eubanks
Copyright © 2005 by W. Ralph Eubanks
Reprinted by permission of Basic Books, a member of Perseus Books Group
Jerry Rice
From *Go Long! My Journey Beyond the Game and the Fame* by Jerry Rice with
    Brian Curtis
Copyright © 2007 by Jerry Rice
Reprinted by permission of Ballantine Books, a division of Random House, Inc.

Photo credits (childhood):
Elizabeth Spencer, courtesy of Elizabeth Spencer
    and University of North Carolina Library
Ellen Douglas, courtesy of Kathie Boatner Blankenstein
Carolyn Haines, by George Day Portrait Studios
Sid Salter, by George Day Portrait Studios

Photo credits (adult):
Richard Ford, © David Hurn/Magnum Photos
Elizabeth Spencer, by John Rosenthal
Ellen Douglas, by Kay Holloway
B. B. King, by Bob Guthridge, copyright © Bob Guthridge 2006,
    www.bobguthridge.com
B. B. King Club, by Charline R. McCord
Elizabeth H. Aydelott, by Charline R. McCord
Donald H. Peterson, courtesy of Donald H. Peterson and NASA
Keith Tonkel, by Greg Campbell Photography, Inc.
Samuel Jones, by T. Gordon Massecar
Noel Polk, courtesy of University Relations, Mississippi State University
Constance Slaughter-Harvey, by Gil Ford Photography, Inc.
Jimmy Buffett, by Pamela Jones
Clifton L. Taulbert, by Bob McCormack Photography, Tulsa
Carolyn Haines, by John Adams
Lorian Hemingway, by Andy Newman/Florida Keys News Bureau
Sid Salter, by Lisa D. McNeece
Wyatt Waters, by Ron Blaylock, www.blaylockphoto.com
Maggie Wade Dixon, by Gil Ford Photography, Inc.
Robert St. John, by Mark Saunders
Jerry Rice, courtesy of Mississippi Valley State University Office of Public Relations

All other photographs are courtesy of the individual essayists.